P9-ASC-213

Bricklaying

A Homeowner's Illustrated Guide

Bricklaying
A Homeowner's Illustrated Guide

Charles R. Self

TAB BOOKS
Blue Ridge Summit, PA

NOTICES
Quikrete®   Quikrete Company
Drylok® and **UGL®**   United Gilsonite Laboratories

FIRST EDITION
FIRST PRINTING

© 1992 by **TAB Books**.
TAB Books is a division of McGraw-Hill, Inc.

Library of Congress Cataloging-in-Publication Data

Self, Charles R.
    Bricklaying : a homeowner's illustrated guide / by Charles R.
  Self.
      p.   cm.
  Includes index.
  ISBN 0-8306-3918-7   ISBN 0-8306-3917-9 (pbk.)
    1. Bricklaying—Amateurs' manuals.   I. Title.
  TH5511.S46 1992
  693'.21—dc20   91-31042
                            CIP

TAB Books offers software for sale. For information and a catalog, please contact TAB Software Department, Blue Ridge Summit, PA 17294-0850.

Acquisitions Editor: Kimberly Tabor
Book Editor: Susan D. Wahlman
Technical Reviewers: Robert L. and Elizabeth Williams
Director of Production: Katherine G. Brown
Book Design: Jaclyn J. Boone   TAB1

Contents

Acknowledgments

This book has taken shape with the help of numerous people, always the case with a do-it-yourself book. Particular thanks are due this time to the Brick Institute of America, Glen-Gery Brick Company, General Shale (Webster Brick Company), and Quikrete Company.

Introduction

*T*he durability of brick construction is almost legendary. During the digging season of 1923–24, Dr. C. L. Wooley of the British University Museum was directing excavations at Ur when workers revealed a ziggurat, a shrine to the moon god, destroyed in about the fifth century B.C. During the clearing of the lowest stages of the building of Ur-Engar, Wooley found a structure, erected about 2300 B.C., approximately 130 by 195 feet in size. Crude brick lined the inside and fine burned brick covered the exterior. The burned exterior brick had been laid with a bitumen mortar. Pitch-soaked reed mats had been placed at regular intervals to provide bonds.

"The quality of these facing bricks and the bricklaying is astonishingly good," Wooley said. "Much of the wall face is as . . . new-looking as when it was first built." Such detail says two important things about brick. First, brick is one of the most durable of all man-made building materials. Second, the production of brick is incredibly ancient. The bricks at Ur present evidence of a long period of development preceding that structure.

Other findings show that brick was in use well before 4000 B.C. Possibly the first use was by some tool-handling early man who happened to notice the way sun-dried clay formed into irregularly cracked blocks. A quick, easy shaping made those adobe blocks into useful building material.

Over time, methods of producing fire-dried, or burned, brick have developed, but basic brick-burning methods are much the same today as they have been for centuries. Clay is mined, then crushed and mixed with water to form a cohesive, thick slurry. Next, the slurry is molded into proper sizes, air-dried for a time, and fired.

Naturally, methods of production have changed with the years, but the essential process works the same today. Modern mechanization brought change that now allows the production of billions of bricks a year. In 1979, over nine billion bricks were manufactured in the United States alone.

While it might seem true that a "brick is a brick," a quick look at the sample bricks at your local building supply outlet will quickly change your mind. The variety of designs, sizes, weights, and uses is amazing. You can now build almost anything with brick, especially in combination with other materials (FIG. A).

A   A great range of wall patterns and surfaces can be achieved by using a wide variety of brick styles and sizes. This mural at Opryland, U.S.A., was carved from brick.

The uses for brick are nearly unlimited, whether simply for decoration or for structural strength. Modern burned brick comes in thousands of different styles, shapes, and colors (FIG. B). It may be used to construct a child's sandbox, a patio, a retaining wall, a decorative wall, (FIG. C), a solid house wall, a veneer house wall, interior floors, or steps. About the only place brick might prove inappropriate is on a ceiling—though even there some of the new thin bricks, about an eighth of the thickness of standard brick, might be worth consideration.

Its beauty is an excellent reason for choosing brick over other materials or as an adjunct to other materials. Another advantage is the fireproofing quality of brick. Brick won't burn in a normal fire because the material has already been heated to 1900 °F. Using brick to build a home will often result in lower fire insurance costs than standard frame construction techniques (FIG. D).

Cost sometimes seems a rational reason to reject brick, but a large portion of the cost of brickwork on or around a house is the price of

B This formal garden illustrates several possible designs and effects that can be created with bricks. Curved surfaces, columns, and decorative touches are possible with careful planning and execution.

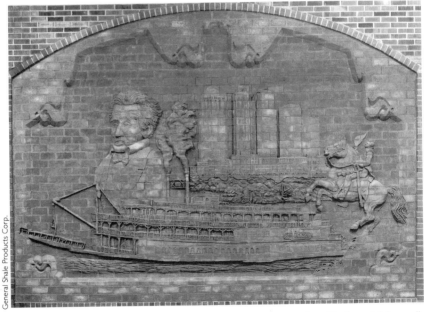

C A wall need not be only a barrier separating rooms or a purely utilitarian retaining wall. Broad ranges of beauty and originality are possible, as this portion of a hotel wall at Opryland, U.S.A., shows.

General Shale Products Corp.

D Brick walls not only reduce insurance rates, they are an integral part of interior decorating, like this wall, corner fireplace, and hearth.

labor. A good brick mason makes an honestly earned decent buck anywhere in the country, and in many areas will do quite well.

While many people view the use of brick as a field only for professionals with extensive training and experience, almost anyone with normal capabilities and a fair amount of care can learn to use this ancient building material. Most people can do brick masonry, but be forewarned: it is not light work by any means. It is satisfying and provides excellent results with only a small amount of practice to develop the needed skills, but the work is physically strenuous and may be fairly dirty at times. However, if you want the safety, durability, and beauty that brick offers, the work is probably worthwhile.

Chapter 1

Brickmaking

*T*he mechanized production of brick today is quite different, in many ways, than it was in the days when workers pressed their fingers in the still damp clay to sign their handmade creations. Plano-convex marked bricks date from 4000 B.C., while special signature stamps, such as those found on the bricks at Ur, came into use around 2250 B.C. In early cases, the making of brick was declared a gift of a particular god, with the entire process of manufacturing often taken under the patronage of the royal monarch of the time.

Brickmaking spread from the Mesopotamian plains into Persia, India, and China, then west to Egypt, Greece, and Rome. Biblical references to building with brick are numerous. Herodotus, a Greek historian of the fifth century B.C., gives an account of the wonders of the Babylonian walls and hanging gardens that Nebuchadnezzar had built with brick. The walls were immense. The inside section was 23 feet thick and made of sun-dried brick. A mud-filled section was 39 feet thick and a facing wall of burned brick was 25 1/2 feet thick. The entire mass, and a mass it was, stood over 365 feet tall.

Europe learned the art of brickmaking from the Romans during the legions' three-and-a-half-century occupation of the continent and England. In England, the practice of brickmaking slid into obscurity until the thirteenth century. During the reign of Henry VIII, brickmaking began to flourish once more. After London burned in 1666, the brick industry grew immensely during the reconstruction. What had been a city built of wood became a city built primarily of brick, far safer from fire. By the eighteenth century, the Georgian influence, with its fine brick country houses, almost ended the use of other forms of building materials.

The first brick used in America was the adobe the Spanish conquistadors found in Peru and Mexico. In Virginia, the brick industry began in 1611. In Massachusetts, brickmaking began in 1629.

Originally, brick was fired by building a small hut from the green brick, then building a fire inside the hut. Real change didn't come until the Industrial Revolution of the last century, although the first brickmaking machine on record predated the nineteenth century. Apollos Kinsley of Connecticut patented a machine that influenced brickmaking for more than 50 years after its patent date of 1793. Kinsley's machine was a vertical mill with an auger to force the clay into molds underneath. The molds were formed clay columns with a small sprue hole in the top to show when the mold was filled. By 1798, an Englishman named Farquharson had patented a more sophisticated version of Kinsley's machine, powered by a horse.

In 1819, near Washington, DC, a horse-powered dry press with a circular pressing table was in operation. Using a single horse, this press was capable of producing brick at the rate of 30,000 per 12-hour day. The number of men required to fill the molds is unknown.

Dry presses were important because in those days, most wet-pressed brick was not ready for the kilns until some of the excess water air-dried out. Since brick often dried in open sheds, production could be lost to weather.

In the 30 years before 1820, the U.S. Patent Office received requests for 21 brickmaking machine patents. Over the next 16 years, the office granted 69 such patents.

By 1862, the extrusion process and the wire cutter had both been invented. The brick industry employs that basic process with little change today. Machine size, power, efficient lubrication, and other factors have vastly improved, and extruded brick is the rule today (FIG. 1-1).

1-1 The invention of the wire cutter and more efficient standardized manufacturing introduced bricks of uniform size and color. The top brick is a patio paver; the bottom is a standard solid brick.

Kilns presented problems during earlier days of brickmaking. Heat conservation in the early models was impossible, raising the cost of brick manufacture. If those inefficient kilns were in use with today's costly energy, few, except the very wealthy, would be able to afford brick as a building material. Continuous or tunnel kilns were first built around 1751. These early kilns had such a great capacity they couldn't be kept in use. This intermittent use cut advantages of heat conservation in the tunnels because the kilns had to be shut down and refired frequently. A circular tunnel kiln was patented by a Swiss engineer in 1857, and a straight-line tunnel kiln was built in 1866, but it wasn't until about 1915 that tunnel kilns really became practical.

Almost all of the basic tools for today's brickmaking were introduced before the turn of the century. Development has continued; efficiency has increased. Today's brick, in relation to inflation, is probably cheaper than at almost any other time in history.

At one time a single town, Haverstraw, on New York's Hudson River, had 54 brick factories. Now no more than a couple hundred survive across the entire country. Brick factories in Haverstraw once took so much clay from the river bank that a large portion of the town slid into the river, killing 10 people.

TYPES OF CLAY

The brick manufacturing process requires clay with enough plasticity to allow shaping or molding when mixed with water. The clay also must have sufficient tensile strength to hold a shape after forming is completed.

Clay comes in three primary forms. Surface clays are upthrusts of older deposits and are found, as their name indicates, near the surface of the earth. In south central Virginia, where I live, I'm surrounded by red surface clay, which is quite fertile if handled correctly (a surprising phenomenon to those, like me, who come from black dirt areas). The red Virginia clay makes for a fine brick industry.

Shales have been subjected to such high pressure that the clay has hardened to almost the consistency of slate. Fire clays, which are found at deeper levels, must be mined. Fire clays are important to fireplace builders and wood-stove manufacturers because they have refractory properties (fire and heat resistance) which keep them from cracking under extreme heat (FIG. 1-2). Generally, fire clays have fewer impurities. All clays have similar chemical compositions even though the physical form may differ markedly. All are compounds of silica and alumina, with varied amounts of metallic oxides and other impurities. The impurities actually act as fluxes, allowing for fusion at lower temperatures.

One of the reasons fire clays ward off the effects of extreme heat so well is their lack of impurities. Fusion occurs at much higher temperatures than for standard brick clay, creating the needed qualities in fire brick.

Iron, magnesium, and calcium oxides have the strongest effect on the color of the finished brick (FIG. 1-3).

General Shale Products Corp.

1-2   The refractory qualities of fire bricks let them withstand intense heat.

General Shale Products Corp.

1-3   In this view of a formal garden, you can see the color variations created by the use of iron, magnesium, and calcium oxides in brick manufacturing.

MANUFACTURING BRICK

The manufacturing process for brick has six stages:

1. winning and storage of raw material
2. preparation of raw material
3. forming units
4. drying
5. burning and cooling
6. drawing and storing the finished units

Winning is the term applied to mining procedures in the clay industry. Common practice is to hold several days' worth of raw materials in storage so that poor weather conditions don't force an expensive shutdown of the equipment.

Preparation involves crushing the clay to break up large chunks, removing stones, and then moving the clay to huge grinding wheels. The grinding wheels weigh from 4 to 8 tons. The clay is ground, mixed, and usually screened in order to control particle sizes and get better uniformity in the final bricks.

Forming starts with tempering to produce a homogeneous plastic mass. In tempering, water is added to the clay in a mill with a mixing chamber. Three processes are used for forming: stiff mud, soft mud, and dry press. In the stiff-mud process, clay is mixed with just enough water to produce plasticity—usually 12%–15% by weight. Once the clay and water are thoroughly mixed (pugged), the clay goes through a de-airing machine with a vacuum of 15–29 inches of mercury. De-airing results in fewer air holes, increased workability, and greater final strength. The clay column is then forced through a die and passed through an automatic cutter. Wire spacings and die sizes are carefully set to allow for normal shrinkage from wet stage through final burning. After leaving the cutting table, units are inspected. Those with imperfections go back to the pugging mill, while the acceptable units are placed on a drying car.

The soft-mud process is used only for the production of brick, while the stiff-mud process can also be used to produce structural clay tile. The soft-mud process is most often used when clays contain too much natural water for the stiff-mud process. Clay is mixed with 20%–30% water, and the units are formed in molds lubricated with sand or water. The soft-mud process is the oldest currently used method of producing brick.

The dry-press process is employed when clays have very low plasticity; it uses a minimum amount of water (no more than 10%). The units are formed in steel molds under pressures ranging from 500 to 1550 pounds per square inch.

When wet clay bricks come from the molding or cutting machines, the water content, by weight, ranges from 7% to 30%, depending on which of the three forming methods has been used. Before burning can begin, most of this water is evaporated in the drier kilns, using temperatures of 100–400 °F. Drying time varies from 24 to 48 hours. Heat for the drier kilns is most often tapped from the waste heat produced by the burning kilns. Heat and humidity are carefully regulated to prevent cracking.

A few bricks, and most tile and terra cotta, are glazed. High-fired glazes are sprayed on the units either before or after drying, and the units are then burned at normal firing temperatures. Low-fired glazes are used when colors would be lost in extreme heat. They are applied after the brick has been burned and cooled. The units are then refired at relatively low temperatures.

Burning requires 40 to 150 hours of the clay unit production time, depending on a number of variables. Dried units are placed in the kiln in a prescribed pattern to permit free circulation of hot air. In tunnel kilns, units are loaded in special cars in a similar manner. Burning divides into six separate stages:

1. water smoking (evaporation of free water)
2. dehydration
3. oxidation
4. vitrification
5. flashing
6. cooling

The first four steps require rising temperatures in the kiln. Water smoking takes place up to 400 °F. Dehydration takes place from 300 to 1800 °F, oxidation from 1000 to 1800 °F, and vitrification from 1600 to 2400 °F.

The rate of temperature change must be carefully controlled. The proper temperature depends on the raw material and the type of unit being produced. Kilns are equipped with recording pyrometers to keep a careful check on the burning process.

Near the end of the burning process, the units may be flashed to change the color. Clays containing iron oxides will burn to a red color when exposed to an oxidizing fire, which allows ferrous oxide to form. Changing the fire to a reducing type will give the units a purplish tinge. This use of a reducing fire is known as flashing.

Cooling is another step that must be carefully controlled. Tunnel kilns will usually allow a finished cooling in about 48 hours or less. Care must be used since a too-rapid cooling will cause excessive cracking. The next step after cooling is drawing, the process of removing the bricks from the kiln. The bricks then are sorted, graded, and stored or shipped.

CHARACTERISTICS OF BRICK

Both the raw materials and the manufacturing process affect the final properties of brick and clay tile. The properties of most concern in these building materials are color, texture, size variation, absorption, compressive strength, and durability. For fire brick, refractory qualities are also important.

The color of burned clay depends on its chemical composition, burning temperatures, and the type of burning control used. Iron has the most effect on color since a normal, or oxidizing, fire always produces a red brick when iron is present in the clay. The higher the temperature of the burning kiln, the darker the color. In addition, brick's compressive strength is increased with the higher temperatures.

Texture can be created by using dies or molds during forming. Smooth brick is called die skin and is a result of the pressure exerted inside the steel die. If the stiff-mud process is used to form the brick, attachments can add cuts, scratches, brush marks, or other textures to the face of the brick as the clay column leaves the die.

Sizing is important since you would naturally like to know, within reasonable limits, just how many bricks you'll need to do a job, and the brickmaker needs to know how many bricks can be produced from specific quantities of raw materials. Different clays shrink at different rates under different conditions. Air shrinkage ranges from 2% to 8%, while fire shrinkage ranges from $2^1/2$% to 10%. Fire shrinkage is greatest at higher temperatures. Total shrinkage can cover a range from $4^1/2$% to 15%.

Compressive strength and absorption are qualities affected by the clay properties, method of manufacture, and degree of burning. Generally, the stiff-mud process will provide units of greater compressive strength and lower absorption than units produced by the other two processes. However, exceptions are possible. Given a particular type of clay, the higher the burning temperature, the greater the compressive strength and the lower the absorption. The type of clay used has a great impact on the final outcome.

So far, I have pretty well covered the manufacture of the most popular types of brick for home and commercial use in the United States. Another form seems to be regaining an imputed former popularity among some groups devoted to natural living. Air-dried, or adobe, brick has often been used for construction by South American and American Southwest natives. Adobe brick requires far less heat energy to produce.

ADOBE BRICK

Essentially, adobe brick is a mixture of claylike mud, finely chopped straw, and water left to dry in the sun. It is more suitable for production and use in those areas of the country, such as the Southwest, where sunny days tend to prevail. At present no one seems to be producing such brick on a large scale, so you'll almost certainly need to do your own adobe brick manufacturing. Molds are used and the actual mixture must be a matter of experimentation. The consistency of the local clay will determine much of the other requirements. The batch must be mixed very well, poured into the molds and allowed to dry in the sun until completely hard. Generally, adobe bricks are larger and heavier than standard brick. Some bricks weigh as much as 40 pounds and few weigh under 20 pounds.

Adobe bricks should be laid using the same mortar you would use for burned brick or concrete block. The same basic techniques are used—with one addition. Adobe is noted for its ability to absorb water. This property can, in rainy areas, quickly reduce a building to little more than a mud lump on your lot. Treatment of some kind is needed to provide water resistance, especially in areas subject to heavy rains or flooding.

A lot of information can be found on the unparalleled insulating qualities of brick—particularly adobe brick. Don't believe too much of that. No solid material such as brick, whether adobe or burned, offers great thermal insulating properties. Generally, a brick or adobe wall would need to be two to three feet thick to equal the insulating properties of a house framed in 2 × 4s, using $3^1/2$ inches of fiberglass insulation between studs. With proper preparation and handling, a brick wall may be designed to provide superb sound and thermal insulation duties, but a single *wythe* (brick width) wall will do neither job well.

BRICK STYLES AND SIZES

Much of the success of a particular bricklaying job depends on the selection of the proper brick size and the correct style to fit both the decor of the area or home and the job at hand. While I can't cover each and every brick style, not to mention special sizes on special orders from brickyards in this book, a good number of constants, including a normal brick size, exist in this field. Note, though, that the actual size of a brick is somewhat less than its standard dimensions.

Standardization in the sizes of building materials is now an accepted rule, though the practice is far from perfect. Since the construction industry in most cases still operates on the English system, without bothering with metrics, you can, for the most part, do the same. It is possible to have your supply house or hardware store order metric, or metric/English measuring equipment from tool makers. But right now, and in the immediate future, what you have should serve.

In most cases, modules run in units of four, either 4 inches or 4 feet. Examples are 16 inches on center framing, 2 feet on center framing and 4-×-8-foot paneling. In the case of bricks, the modules are 4 inches, though the actual brick is smaller. If it weren't, the mortar would make the module oversized. Standard bricks are nominally sized at $2^1/2 × 4 × 8$ inches, while their actual size is $2^1/2 × 3^5/8 × 7^5/8$ inches. With such sizing, the brick manufacturers allow you to place a $3/8$-inch thickness of mortar on three sides of the brick.

This size is a basic brick, and many, many variations occur from maker to maker. Variations also occur within a particular batch of bricks, since materials will vary, as will burning time and other factors. Also, the likelihood of variation in size from one maker to another is strong. It usually pays to buy all the brick for a particular job from the same manufacturer. Also, try to buy all the brick in a single lot, as this method comes closest to ensuring the greatest consistency.

In the United States, the standard brick is $2^{1}/_{2} \times 3^{3}/_{4} \times 8$ inches, while English bricks are $3 \times 4^{1}/_{2} \times 9$ and Roman bricks are $1^{1}/_{2} \times 4 \times 12$ inches. Norman bricks are $2^{3}/_{4} \times 4 \times 12$ inches. These are the standard brick styles and sizes, but bricks are also available in other classifications. One of those classifications is *building brick*.

Building brick was formerly known as common brick. Made of standard clay or shale, it has no special markings, color, or surface texture. This type of brick is most commonly used for the backing courses in solid and cavity brick walls.

Face brick is most frequently used for exposed surfaces because they are of higher quality than building bricks, with better durability and better appearance. Face brick is usually available in a variety of shades of red, brown, gray, yellow, and white, with many patterns and textures.

For rough work where great durability is important, you can ask for *clinker brick*. Clinker brick is the result of overburning in the kilns. Frequently not regularly shaped, clinker brick is sometimes called roughhard.

Pressed brick is made with the dry-press process. It has regular, smooth faces; sharp edges; and perfectly square corners. It is almost always used as face brick.

For fancier applications, you can buy *glazed brick* in a variety of colors. One face is coated with a ceramic glaze of mineral ingredients which fuse together to produce a smooth, glasslike surface when the brick is burned. Such bricks are used where a smooth, easily cleaned, and attractive surface is desired. The use of glazed brick can save the cost of covering walls with ceramic tile.

Fire brick is used for lining fireplaces, woodstoves, and barbecues. Although most people don't bother to line barbecues, their durability can be greatly increased if fire brick is used. As I mentioned earlier in this chapter, this type of brick, made from deep-mined fire clay of greater purity than other clays, is strongly resistant to the effects of heat. It requires much greater temperatures to achieve fusion, which makes the brick harder and less likely to crack and crumble under heating and cooling cycles. Fire brick is larger than standard brick, with a nominal size depending on the maker (FIG. 1-4).

Most fireplaces installed today have metal liners instead of fire brick. They reduce the need for a lot of work and add the possibility of increasing fireplace efficiency. Today, no one at all serious about wood heat should even consider using an unmodified fireplace. Even most of those that are modified are not nearly as efficient as a good modern wood stove. At the same time, fireplaces lined with metal are not as durable as those lined with fire brick. Some fireplace inserts now take advantage of the fire brick in the fireplace (FIG. 1-5).

Most types of brick can also be obtained in what is known as the *cored brick* style. Basically, cored brick has either three holes in a single row up the center or two rows of five holes each. This core removal does little more than cut the weight of the bricks, since no appreciable differ-

General Shale Products Corp.

1-4 Sizes of fire bricks can vary considerably; the nominal dimensions depend on the individual producers. Even a very hot fire, such as the one shown here, will have little or no effect on the consistency and integrity of the bricks.

General Shale Products Corp.

1-5 Fireplace inserts are both popular and effective. They can reduce heat loss and circulate heated air by way of a blower system. Wood bins provide attractive storage areas for fuel.

ence in strength or resistance to moisture penetration is apparent between cored and uncored bricks. Coring does reduce any chance of using the wide surface of the brick for facing, whether as a paver or another type of face brick. Use whatever type—cored or uncored—is most readily available in the most suitable style, color, and texture for the job at hand.

Occasionally, you might run into some types of imported brick. *European brick*, especially from England and Holland, can compare favorably with American clay brick in strength and durability. The price will probably seem excessive unless only a few bricks are needed. More rarely, you might find *sand-lime brick*. These bricks, most extensively used in Germany, are made from a thin mixture of slaked lime and very fine siliceous sand molded under pressure and hardened by steam.

STRENGTH

A great deal of strength in any bricklaying job depends on the mortar used, but other important factors must be considered. The strength of the individual brick is crucial. Well-burned bricks frequently exceed a compressive strength of 15,000 pounds per square inch. The workmanship of the bricklayer also has much to do with the final job strength. For that reason, place much emphasis on care in every aspect of the bricklaying job, starting with the first, basic plan of the job through mixing the mortar and laying the brick.

If the brick is not uniform, the strength of the job will be decreased. Keep an eye on the load as it is delivered and as you go through the pile. Order enough extra bricks to make sure you can set aside the ones seriously out of conformity with the rest of the batch.

The method used in laying the brick—here I mean the type of bond used, not necessarily the workmanship—has a great impact on job strength. Bonding is covered more thoroughly in chapter 2. It has at least three different meanings when applied to brick masonry, but here I am using the term to mean the pattern in which the bricks are laid, one upon the other.

Certain types of brick are fairly porous and are known as high-suction bricks. If these bricks are not wetted down before being laid, they will suck moisture into the brick from the mortar more rapidly than the mortar can cure and form the mortar bond, seriously weakening the structure. Such bricks must be dampened before use.

FIRE RESISTANCE

Tests have been conducted on brick walls with Portland-lime mortar (recommended for greatest strength in almost every job). The tests show great fire resistance under the normal testing standards of the American Society for Testing Materials (ASTM). With only a single brick four inches thick and with no plaster, fire resistance is $1^1/4$ hours. TABLE 1-1 shows the resistance of other wall thicknesses, with and without plaster on one or two sides of the wall.

Table 1-1   Fire Resistance of Brick Walls

Normal wall thickness (inches)	Type of wall	Material	Ultimate fire-resistance period (hours)		
			No plaster	*Plaster on one side**	*Plaster on two sides**
4	Solid	Clay or shale	$1^1/4$	$1^3/4$	$2^1/2$
8	Solid	Clay or shale	5	6	7
12	Solid	Clay or shale	10	10	12
8	Hollow rowlock	Clay or shale	$2^1/2$	3	4
12	Hollow rowlock	Clay or shale	5	6	7
9 to 10	Cavity	Clay or shale	5	6	7
4	Solid	Sand-lime	$1^3/4$	$2^1/2$	3
8	Solid	Sand-lime	7	8	9
12	Solid	Sand-lime	10	10	12

*Not less than 1/2 inch of 1:3 sanded gypsum plaster is required to develop these ratings.

I can vouch that in real-life situations, bricks resist fire and heat well. In my 155-year-old house, a fire broke out in the predawn hours, starting in the living room of the two-story structure. When I awoke and entered the bathroom, I realized that the room above the living room was in flames. The bedroom in which I slept was, despite the fire raging downstairs, still clear of flames and smoke.

The 13-inch brick wall that separated the living room from the remainder of the house resisted the fire so well that later the entire house was refloored and remodeled. A frame house would have been totally destroyed by the fire.

Many similar stories have been documented in which brick fire walls or separators prevented flames from spreading to other parts of buildings. It is not uncommon to see a massive chimney standing where a house burned down. When flames destroyed the house, the chimney and fireplace were left intact, with no discernible structural damage.

In other instances, brick walls have been left standing after fire had gutted the interior walls. Bricks used as makeshift grates in fireplaces endure dozens of intensely hot fires for hours.

INSULATING PROPERTIES

The thermal insulating properties of brick are not great. Insulation normally depends on a layer, or layers, of unmoving air. Once the air molecules move, they can transmit heat. If a solid, or unframed, brick wall is to be used, it should have a cavity in which insulation can be inserted. Otherwise, the brick wall should be backed by a framed, insulated wall. This technique is known as brick veneering (FIG. 1-7).

The massiveness of a full brick wall provides good sound insulation. However, testing shows that increasing the size of a wall to more than a foot thick is pointless. The sound is not muffled appreciably more once

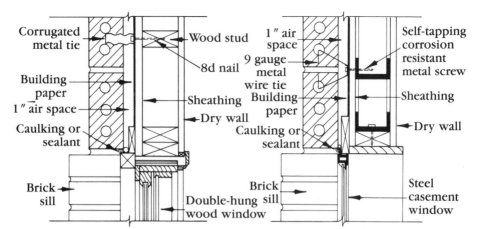

I-6 Brick veneering can be more heat efficient than solid brick walls, but you must make good use of metal ties, sheathing, caulk, building paper, and air spaces. On the left is a detail of the jamb for brick veneer over a wood frame backup wall; on the right, a metal stud backup wall. Brick Institute of America

the wall has reached a thickness of 10 inches. The use of *cavity walls*, as recommended for walls to be insulated, will cut down on sound transmission at lower cost. An added advantage is lower heat loss. While sound transmission through brick walls is low, sound originating inside a brick-walled building (surfaced, at least, with brick on the interior) will rebound quite well. Sound deadening is not a quality of brick. Impact sounds, which result from an object striking the wall, travel far along a brick wall.

As with every construction material, brick and mortar will expand and contract with changing temperatures. Therefore, walls more than a few hundred feet long will probably need expansion joints. However, very few homeowners will be working with such long structures.

Abrasion resistance of brick is related to compressive strength, which is increased by proper burning. If brick is to be used as floor—as an outdoor patio, for example—it should be well burned for greatest durability. Solid brick, depending on the clay used and the degree of burning, will weigh anywhere from 100 to 150 pounds per cubic foot. Generally, the heavier the brick, the better burned it is.

Chapter **2**

Basic bricklaying

Doing a good job of bricklaying depends on many things other than just the quality and style of the brick. For the homeowner, too many worries about working efficiency may be self-defeating. Often you must not only cart your own bricks to the point of construction, but also mix your own mortar, soak the bricks, set any needed ladders or scaffolding, and lay the bricks. The professional brick-layer usually has a helper to assist with such jobs.

Some steps toward increasing efficiency will help. Keep the Portland cement under cover, and keep it as close as possible to your sand and lime piles. Both sand and lime must be well protected against inclement weather. The lime will cake when wetted and dried. Overly wet sand makes getting a properly elastic mortar mix difficult.

Most people working with bricks and mortar use some sort of wheel-barrow as a mixing unit (FIG. 2-1). Mortar trays also work well (FIG. 2-2). Don't mix any more mortar than you will need at one time. If you want good results, don't use partially set-up mortar. A single sack of premixed mortar will be sufficient for approximately 50 bricks. To mix your mortar, you can use an ordinary garden hoe, or buy a special mortar hoe with a thicker blade and holes for the mortar to pass through (FIG. 2-3). A source of water nearby is a help, but buckets and hoses will work if no tap is close. Keeping tools and mixing tubs as free as possible of partially dried mortar will also help.

Frequent clean-up will add to the time needed to complete the job, reducing apparent efficiency but increasing durability by a large factor. Keeping the work area cleared and clean also contributes to safety.

If you will need scaffolding, plan ahead and gather materials before work begins. (See appendix B for more information on using scaffolding.) Be very careful while working on any type of platform or scaffold. It may

2-1   You can use a wheelbarrow, rather than a mortar pan or box, to mix small amounts of mortar or concrete.

2-2   Metal trays are very useful for mixing mortar. Rounded corners help you achieve a complete mix because dry mix and fine aggregates can be pulled into the mixture easily.

not seem all that dangerous, and it usually isn't, but special care is necessary whenever you are working above ground level.

If bricks are stacked along a wall in amounts you need, you will save a great deal of work time. Bricks weigh more than 100 pounds per cubic foot and mortar is also heavy. If you use some sort of platform to hold the bricks and mortar supply as the wall, chimney, or other project rises, you might avoid backache from bending and lifting. I recently completed an

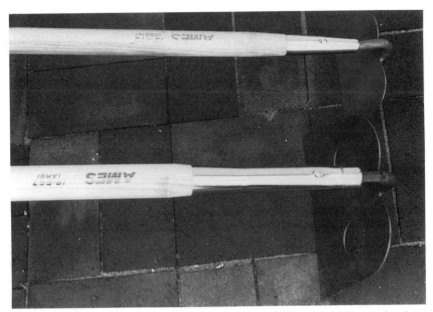

2-3 Mixing hoes are stronger, thicker, and more helpful than ordinary garden hoes, although the latter may be used if you are mixing small amounts of mortar. The holes in the mortar hoe allow the mixture to slide through the hoe.

indoor decorative chimney where I did not have enough room to work in such a manner. By the time the chimney was 7 feet tall, my resulting pain was made bearable only by the overall change in the looks of the room.

BONDS

Most of us tend to interpret the word *bond* as simply meaning how well the mortar holds the bricks or other units together. Actually, three types of bonds apply to brick masonry.

The first bond is *structural bond*, the method by which individual masonry units are interlocked so that the entire structure acts as a single assembly. Without this bond, your structure would topple at the first hint of high wind or at a sharp blow. Structural bonds are accomplished in three ways. Overlapping or interlocked masonry units is one method. In the second method, metal ties are embedded in connecting joints. In the third method, grout is adhered to an adjacent horizontal masonry wall.

The *mortar bond*—the adhesion of the joint mortar to the brick tiles, cement block, or any reinforcements such as veneer wall brick tiles—is as important to structural integrity as the structural bond.

The *pattern bond* is simply the pattern the bricks and mortar joints form in the face of the wall. It might or might not be related to the structural bond method used. In other words, the pattern bond might be an integral part of the overall structural integrity of the wall, or it might simply be a decorative bond with other methods used to form a good structural bond. Essentially, the five basic pattern bonds are *running bond*, *common (American) bond, Flemish bond, English bond*, and *stack bond*. Figure 2-4 shows several types of bonds in addition to the patterns for the five basics.

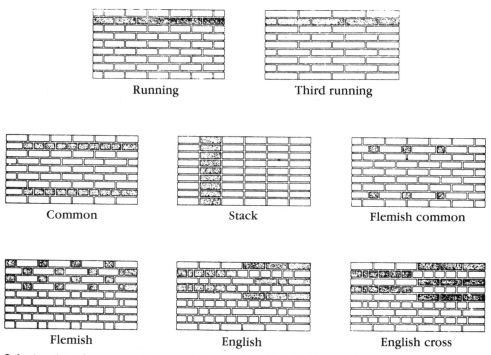

Running   Third running

Common   Stack   Flemish common

Flemish   English   English cross

2-4 A variety of masonry patterns and bonds can be achieved with good planning and execution.

Running bonds are the simplest for the layman to use, since all *stretcher bricks* are used. Each brick runs halfway across the next brick. The running bond is often used with metal ties for veneer walls. It also is a handy bond for cavity wall construction. A variation is the one-third running bond, which uses a longer-than-standard brick, with one upper *course* brick overlapping one-third of the stretcher length. The next brick covers the final two-thirds of the lower course brick. Either type of running bond is fairly easy to lay. This method requires only minimal advance planning and layout to get everything exact.

Common, or American, bond is a variation on the running bond. Instead of all stretchers, a course of *headers*—bricks turned sideways with the end showing in the course—is added at intervals. For example, a course of headers could be placed on the third course up, another on the eighth course up, another on the eleventh course, and so on. The common bond is a bit harder to work out and lay than the running bond alone, but the header courses provide a full structural bond either to brick ties or to the second section of a cavity wall. The structural needs will often determine the header course pattern. Some walls might need a header course every fourth row, while others will not need headers more than every seventh course or so. *Starter brick* for header bond are known as three-quarters, so bricks must be cut for this type of bond.

Flemish bond offers both a structural and decorative option,—as does common bond, which may be done in the same manner. With Flemish bond, headers are used as alternates to stretchers on every course. The headers are centered over the stretchers in the course below. For purely decorative use, bricks may be cut in half and used as headers. For structural use, they may be left whole and tied into either a second wall, for cavity wall construction, or to metal brick ties for veneering. Half bricks or *closures* used in this way are called *blind headers*. You can use two different methods of starting the header courses in Flemish bond. Using three-quarters of a brick is called the Dutch method, while using a 2-inch (quarter-brick) closure is known as the English method.

English bond uses alternating courses of headers and stretchers, but differs from American bond in that the headers are centered on the stretchers and the joints between the stretchers line up vertically. Blind headers may be used in any course which has no need for structural bonding.

Block or stack bond is purely and simply a pattern bond. It offers little structural strength, since all vertical joints are aligned. In most cases, rigid steel ties are essential to structural integrity when using stack bond. However, it is possible to buy and use 8-inch stretchers to add the needed strength. Even with the 8-inch stretchers or steel ties, if the wall is to be large and load bearing, steel pencil rods are needed to provide appropriate strength. These pencil rods are inserted in the horizontal mortar joints. For the best appearance with stack bond, you'll need to select carefully the bricks to be used. They must be closely matched to make this geometric pattern attractive.

The English cross or Dutch bond is a variation of the straight English bond. It differs only in that the vertical joints between the stretchers in alternate rows don't line up. Instead, the vertical joints center on the stretchers both above and below.

MASONRY TERMS

A further description of some of the vocabulary used in masonry work might well be in order. Brick *masonry* is essentially the construction of almost any project using units of baked clay or shale in a uniform size that are laid in courses with mortar joints to form the structural units. Cut brick is named by shape, with the half brick also known as a *bat*. Cut bricks include *three-quarter* and *quarter closures*, *king closure* (cut at an angle across one corner), *queen closure* (cut in half lengthwise) and *split*, which, as its name implies, is a half-brick split up the middle (FIG. 2-5).

Brick surfaces also have appropriate names, as FIG. 2-6 shows.

A *course* is nothing more than one of a continuing row of bricks, which, when bonded to other courses, forms the basic masonry structure (FIG. 2-7).

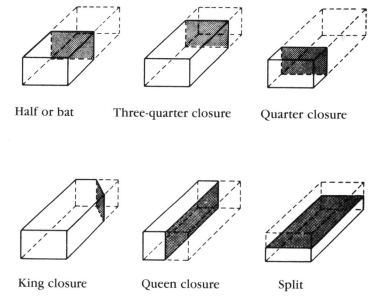

Half or bat   Three-quarter closure   Quarter closure

King closure   Queen closure   Split

2-5 Cut bricks are used to fill corners and other spaces where a full brick won't fit.

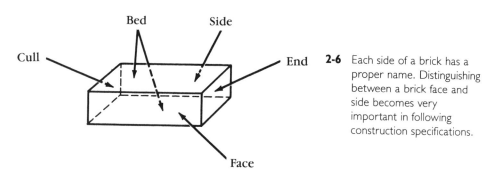

2-6 Each side of a brick has a proper name. Distinguishing between a brick face and side becomes very important in following construction specifications.

A *wythe* is a continuous vertical, 3 inches or wider, section or thickness of masonry. Probably the best example is the wythe surrounding a chimney to keep *flues* separated. A *stretcher* is a brick laid flat with the longest part parallel to the face of the structure being built.

A *header* is a brick laid flat with its longest side perpendicular to the face of the unit under construction. Headers are most often used to tie two wythes of masonry together, but extra-length headers may also be used to form a cavity wall.

A *rowlock* is a brick laid on its face. A *bull stretcher* is a brick laid with its longest side parallel to the face of the wall. A *bull header* is a rowlock brick laid with its longest side perpendicular to the face of the wall. A *soldier* is a brick laid on its end so that its longest dimension is parallel to the vertical mortar joints of the wall.

Flashing is almost always made of metal, usually aluminum. It is used to move moisture away from spots where the masonry is particularly vul-

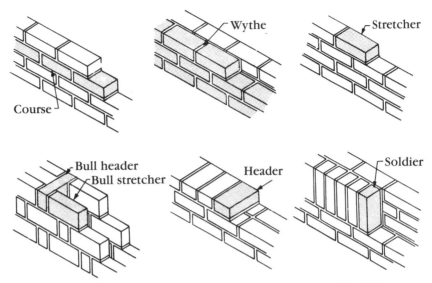

2-7 Masonry units are identified according to the placement of the bricks.

nerable to penetration by water. Generally, flashing is used under horizontal masonry surfaces such as sills, where masonry walls intersect with the roof and other such surfaces (around the chimney base, for example), over door header openings and window headers, and sometimes along floor lines. Flashing extends through the outer face of the wall and is turned down, with weep holes provided every 16 to 24 inches so any water that pools on the flashing can drain. Regardless of the requirements of appearance, flashing should extend beyond the face of the wall. Concealed or partially concealed flashing could concentrate wetness, harming structural integrity.

BASIC MORTAR JOINTS

Later I'll go into further detail on mixing mortar (chapter 3) and the layout of more complex brick structures, but one of the most important techniques to learn in brick masonry is laying and tooling the basic mortar joint. Holding the trowel correctly—when working space permits—is a help. The thumb does not, and should not, encircle the trowel grip (FIG. 2-8). The trowel is generally pointed down and away from the body. If you are right-handed, you will use the left edge of the trowel to pick up your mortar from the outside of the mortar pile (FIG. 2-9). Pick up enough mortar to cover no more than three bricks at the outset. Even less mortar is better for the novice. Picking up enough for a single brick forms a small row of mortar along the left side of the trowel, while enough mortar for five bricks loads up the standard-sized trowel.

The left edge of the trowel is held directly over the center of the course of bricks, tilted, and the mortar drops into place as the trowel is moved to the right. Any mortar remaining on the trowel is tapped back

2-8   To keep a proper grip on the trowel, rest your thumb on the handle rather than wrapping it around the handle.

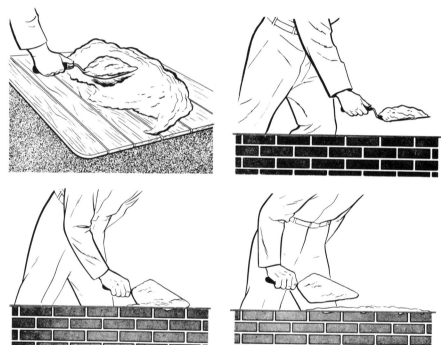

2-9   Pick up enough mortar to cover three to five bricks.

onto a mortar board for later use, not onto the course of bricks. Instead of working from left to right, a left-handed bricklayer simply reverses the direction of these procedures. Any mortar hanging over the edges of the brick is scraped off and returned to the mortar board.

The *bed*, or *base, joint* is spread with about an inch of mortar. Make a shallow furrow, tapering from the center to the outsides (FIG. 2-10), butter the end of the first brick, and push it into the mortar. The furrow must be shallow. If you make it too deep, the gap left between the mortar and the brick will allow for excessive moisture penetration. Eventually, and especially in exterior construction, the joint will break up and lose its bond. Mortar for the bed joint should be spread no more than five bricks along

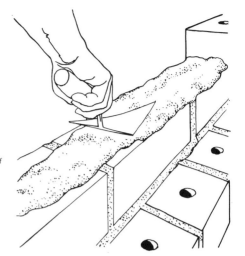

2-10 When the mortar is spread, make a furrow with the tip or point of the trowel. Brick Institute of America

the course. Mortar that is spread too far dries too rapidly, cutting the bonding properties. If the mortar isn't soft and plastic, scrape it up, clean the bed and restart your bed joint. Any mortar that has dried this much should not be returned to the mortar board.

When brick is picked up to be bedded in the mortar, your thumb will be on one side and your fingers on the other. The brick is held with one end hanging down, and the top end is buttered (FIG. 2-11). *Buttering* means pushing as much mortar on the end of the brick as will stick. If you don't get enough mortar on the end of the brick, your *head joint* (vertical joint) will not be full. Push the brick hard enough to force mortar out of the head joint. Then cut off the excess mortar (FIG. 2-12) and return it to the mortar board. If the mortar is setting up a bit, but not a lot, it may be set on the back of the mortar board for *retempering* (see chapter 3).

2-11 Hold a brick with your fingers on one side, your thumb on the other, and butter the end with mortar.

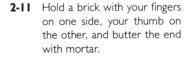

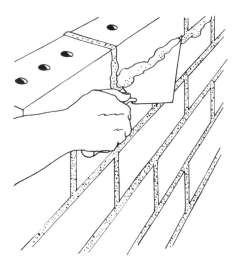

2-12 Cut off the excess mortar forced out at the joints and return it to the pan to use later. Brick Institute of America

A mason's line is used to correctly position the bricks horizontally. Experienced brick masons will often use such a guide only every 8 or 10 courses, but novices should run the line after two courses have been laid. If you have trouble keeping the course horizontal, move the cord after each course is down. It might seem fussy and a waste of time, but in the end, the results will be well worth the extra time taken. Vertical wall plumb can be held with a plumb bob on a cord or with a level used after every few courses. Actually, the level may be used to hold the horizontal line, too, but the line is a bit easier and quicker to use in most cases, especially on long courses where you can move along without checking the level of every two or three bricks.

Occasionally, you might need to insert a single brick in a space in the wall. To achieve a good bond all around, be sure to lay a thick bed of mortar on the bottom of the hole and on the sides. Then lay a thick buttering of mortar on the top of the brick and shove it into place. When the brick is shoved to its final position, you should find mortar squeezed out of each joint, including the top, bottom, and both headers (FIG. 2-13). The excess mortar is, as always, scraped off.

For joining wythes, you'll need to make *cross joints* in header courses (FIG. 2-14). Particularly if the header course aids in structural integrity, you must make certain these cross joints are full of mortar. The entire side of the brick must be thickly buttered before being butted against the preceding brick. Even if the structural integrity of the wall is not essential, any joint not filled completely with mortar will soon allow excessive penetration of moisture, which can break up a brick wall in climates that are subject to freeze and thaw cycles—as most areas of this country are. Excess mortar might squeeze out the top of this header course. Again, any excess on the face and top is cut off.

As you finish a header course, you probably will have a single brick gap waiting to be filled. Instead of buttering the end of the brick you hold in your hand, butter the ends of the bricks already in place to a thickness

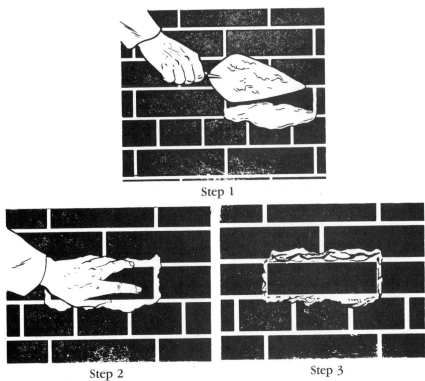

Step 1

Step 2   Step 3

2-13 When you need to lay a single brick inside an existing wall, spread mortar in the hole and then butter the top of the brick. Insert the brick and cut away excess mortar.

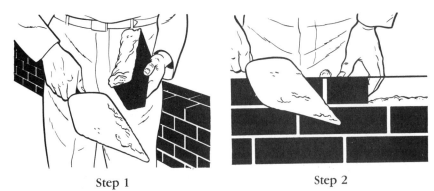

Step 1   Step 2

2-14 If you are laying a cross joint in a header course, butter the side of the brick and push it into place, then cut away mortar that is pressed out of the joints.

of at least 1 inch. Then place a bed of mortar on the lower course, if it isn't already in place, and insert the closure brick. Try your best not to disturb the bricks already in place (FIG. 2-15).

To close a stretcher course, the closure brick is treated like the closure brick for a header course, with one extra step. Butter both ends of

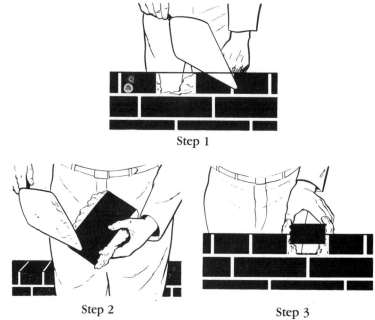

Step 1

Step 2

Step 3

2-15 When laying the final brick in a header course, butter the inside edges of the bricks already in place. You also can butter the brick about to be inserted.

the closure brick as thickly as possible, and cover the ends of the bricks already in place. Again, do your best not to disturb the bricks already laid. Any disturbance means those bricks must be removed, cleaned and relaid. If the bricks are disturbed and not relaid, the bond will be poor and the joints could open and allow water penetration.

One of the most difficult factors for the novice bricklayer to determine is how thick the mortar joints should be. Much depends, of course, on the uniformity of the brick being laid, because the irregularities of the brick are taken up by the mortar joint. The more regular the brick, the thinner the mortar joint. The optimum bonding, assuming the mortar is correctly mixed, occurs with a quarter-inch joint. With irregular bricks, a joint thickness of up to a half inch is acceptable and will provide good strength.

Immediately after each course is laid, pick up your jointing tool and compact the mortar in the joints by the process called *pointing*. Pointing gently forces the tool into the joint and draws it along to compact the mortar even more than it already has been (FIG. 2-16). In some cases, extra mortar must be added to get a clean-looking joint. (When old brick walls are repaired, the job is also called pointing. See appendix A for more information on repairing brick masonry.)

CUTTING BRICK

Often a brick must be cut, as in the case of a half brick for header courses or a quarter brick for English bonds. A brick chisel is the most accurate

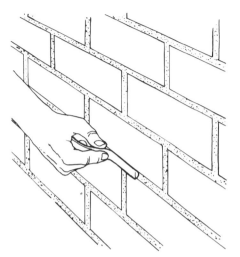

2-16 When the mortar becomes thumbprint-hard, use a jointing tool to pack the mortar joints for better weather resistance.
Brick Institute of America

tool for any such cutting (FIG. 2-17). Score the brick with the chisel at the cutting point (FIG. 2-18). Set the chisel (or *bolster*) on the scribed line and give it a sharp rap with a mason's hammer. Keep the straight side of the cutting edge of the chisel facing the portion of the brick that is to be used.

2-17 Cut bricks using a masonry hammer and a brick chisel (or bolster). Hold the chisel on the cut line and hit it sharply with the hammer.

Brick hammers also have cutting edges for brick since some bricks are too hard to be cut accurately with a chisel. The brick hammer is used to chip away the brick until the scored line is reached (FIG. 2-19). The brick chisel is used for the final trim cut.

2-18   The scored line on the near edge of the brick marks the point of the chisel cut. Hold the chisel so that the straight side of the cutting edge is facing the part of the brick that is to be used.

2-19   Use the brick hammer to chip away any irregularities after the cut is made.

A masonry cut-off wheel, designed to fit an electric drill or electric saw, can also be used to cut bricks. You can buy a masonry wheel for electric saws at any hardware store. These work very well but create a great deal of dust. Use protective glasses or goggles and cut outdoors or in a well-ventilated place.

As with all power tools, exert great care and put safety first. If you must use a masonry blade indoors, you will need to cover furniture and curtains. You will also need to wear a protective mask to prevent inhalation of brick dust.

JOINT FINISHING

Joints must be tooled for two basic reasons: appearance and strength. Compacted mortar in the joint creates a stronger bond. Joints cut flush may crack and permit water to seep into the joint. There the water may freeze and thaw and eventually damage the wall.

Because most amateurs work at a slower pace than professional brick masons, you will need to tool the joints as you build the structure. The mortar joint compresses best and finishes more easily while the mortar is still rather plastic. Usually a jointing tool is used for the purpose, although other items, depending on the shape you want or need, may be used. At times I've used a fingertip, but I don't really recommend it for more than about 3 feet of joint unless you're trying to remove your fingerprints. At other times, the basic blunt end of a toothbrush handle has given the desired shape. Experiment a bit if you don't care for the joint shape your jointing tool gives you.

Essentially, three types of tooled joints are made in brick masonry. The concave joint is the best joint from the standpoint of sealing the mortar against water penetration and the effects of the weather. First, cut off all excess mortar with your trowel. Next, select the jointing tool with the shape you desire. Several shapes are available, including square-ended, V-ended, and curved. The tool tip should be slightly wider than the joint being worked. Use just enough force to press the mortar tightly against the brick on both sides of the joint. Carry your movement along the joint as smoothly as possible. I prefer to do the vertical joints first because that tends to make a cleaner line along the horizontal joints in most kinds of bonds. You might prefer a more broken look.

In the flush joint, excess mortar is cut off nearly level with the face of the wall. Use the tip of the trowel at a position slightly away from parallel with the face of the joint. The angle should be about 10 to 15 degrees, depending on the effect you prefer. Draw the trowel tip along the joint. The resulting joint is not as tightly packed as the concave joint and therefore is less resistant to water penetration.

For a weather joint, excess mortar is cut away with the trowel. The joint is formed by pushing down on the remaining mortar with the top edge of the trowel. While this joint is effective at shedding water running down the face of the brick, it is a much worse joint finish to use in situations where large quantities of water might be blown up against the face of the wall.

The methods described in this chapter present some of the basics of working with brick. From here on, things will get a bit more complicated as I tell you how to work out a good mortar mix and show you what's needed for the base, or footing, under most types of brickwork. You must know not only what happens with mortar, but also what kind of concrete or concrete block is needed to support a durable and attractive brick structure.

Chapter **3**

Concrete
and mortar

You need to know at least a bit about concrete before moving on to mortar and bricklaying on a more extensive basis. The reasons are quite simple. First, Portland cement is used to make mortar. Second, concrete is used either for footings for brickwork or for footings for concrete block that supports brickwork.

Concrete in its usable form has plasticity. It is readily molded but changes shape rather slowly when the mold is removed. The speed of that shape change is influenced by the mix of the concrete. The quality and character of the finished product is also strongly affected by the mix. The degree of plasticity affects the workability of the concrete. Concrete with a very stiff mix is needed for certain types of work, but such stiffness would be out of place where the concrete mix had to flow into heavily reinforced sections or into smaller openings in forms. Workability is primarily controlled by the amounts and proportion of fine to coarse aggregates used with a given quantity of concrete paste (water and pure concrete).

Uniformity of mix is essential for greatest overall strength. Each batch should meet the same specifications as the first.

Naturally, strength is important. One of the basic reasons for using concrete is its great compressive strength. The ratio of water to cement is the basic factor that influences final mix strength. However, other variables must also be controlled. Hydration (drying) time is partly controlled by the amount of water added at the outset. It may also be controlled by keeping the mix damp and curing it for various lengths of time. Each sack of cement needs about $2^1/2$ gallons of water to obtain the proper chemical drying action that takes place when cement cures. The thinner the paste after this point, the weaker the final result. Generally, making each sack of cement workable requires a minimum of 4 gallons of water and a maximum of 8 gallons. The amount depends on just how damp the fine and coarse aggregates—sand and gravel—are when you mix the concrete. Simply dumping in so many gallons of water per so many pounds of dry mix doesn't always work. For greatest watertightness, the Army Corps of Engineers recommends using no more than 6 gallons of water per sack of cement. Durability decreases when too much water is used in the mix.

Portland cements are mixtures of raw materials, finely ground, heated to a fusion temperature of about 2700°F, and finely ground again. When combined with water, Portland cements harden through hydration to form a rock-hard mass. In general, most residential concrete work will be done with ASTM Type 1 Portland Cement. ASTM provides categories for other types of Portland cements, but they are of little general interest. ASTM Type 1 Portland cement is classified as a general cement for use where special properties, such as high resistance to certain acids or low-heat drying, are not needed. Uses include pavement of all kinds, reinforced concrete buildings, bridges, tanks, culverts, masonry units, soil cement mixtures, and mortars.

The only essential requirement for storing Portland cement is to keep it dry. If it is kept dry, the cement will last indefinitely. Moisture contact may set it in a mass or cause it to set more slowly when used, with lower resulting strength.

Water used in making cement should be as pure and clean as possible. In most cases water that is fit to drink is pure enough to make cement. However, if your area is one where excessive sulfates are found in the water, the water should not be used to mix concrete, even though it is classed as fit to drink.

AGGREGATES

The characteristics of aggregates, which make up 60%−80% of the final dry mix, used in concrete work have a great effect on the final product. Rough-textured aggregates require more water to produce workable concrete than do smoother particles. With rough aggregates, more cement must also be added to keep the water-cement ratio in balance for the correct final strength.

Aggregates range from fine mason's sand to large gravel, crushed stone, cinders, and, on occasion, burned clay. The result, with a proper mix, is concrete that weighs from 135 to 160 pounds per cubic foot. Aggregates should be as free of contamination as possible. Some types may be washed to get rid of dirt, organic material, salts, and other contaminates. Sand which contains organic materials cannot be decontaminated. In most areas of the country, simply buying good mason's sand will ensure the quality you need. The same is true for good bank-run gravel that is washed and sized for a particular job. At times, and in some areas, good aggregate may be hard to come by and more costly than seems reasonable. But it simply doesn't make sense to do your work with less than the best materials available for the job, if you expect excellent results.

Grading

Aggregates are graded for resistance to abrasion, resistance to freezing and thawing, and chemical stability. Particle shape, size, and texture are also important. Generally, you're safe using whatever type of sand and gravel local contractors prefer. Most reputable contractors look for quality as well as low cost.

Grading for size depends on the type of work you are doing. When, as with brick masonry, your major concern is a footing or a footing and base wall to support brick work, the largest coarse aggregate used should be no more than a quarter of the thickness of the unit being constructed. In other words, if you're pouring an 8-inch footing, the largest piece of coarse aggregate should be no more than 2 inches across. In no case should coarse aggregate exceed $2^1/_2$ inches in diameter.

Cleanliness

With aggregate of any kind, assuming that the basic quality is good, cleanliness also needs to be considered. If you have any doubts about the cleanliness of your aggregate, run a silt test. Take a quart jar and place about 2 inches of the aggregate in the bottom. Fill the jar with water and give it a gentle shake. Let it stand until the aggregate settles and then check the depth of the silt on top of the aggregate. If you find more than about $1/_8$ inch of silt, wash the aggregate before you use it (FIG. 3-1).

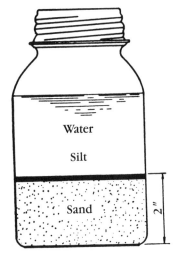

3-1 The quart-jar method shows the silt content of sand.

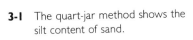

To wash the aggregate, drive a pickup-truckload of the material to a gentle grade and park the truck nose-up. Use a hose to run water into the truck bed over the aggregate. Keep the water running in a steady stream until the water that drains out the back of the truck runs clear. At this point the aggregate should be clean enough for satisfactory use.

You will not have a huge load of gravel in the truck bed because its weight is great, even for relatively small amounts, so washing each load of aggregate will not take very long. Fifteen minutes is usually sufficient.

Let the washed aggregate continue to drain as long as you can. If possible, place the aggregate in the sun to dry for several hours. You can use wet aggregate for concrete, but for mortar you should use dry aggregate.

Testing for organic matter in aggregate is sometimes necessary. Place about one measuring cup of the suspect aggregate into a quart jar. If the aggregate is sand, and you suspect the presence of organic material, do the test before making the purchase. Add a cup of clean water and one heaping teaspoon of household lye. Don't use the type of lye in drain cleaners as these contain aluminum chips that interfere with the testing. Use plain old lye and nothing else. Shake well, though gently, until the lye is completely dissolved.

Set the jar aside for 24 hours and then take a look at the color of its contents. If the color is orange, organic material is present. If it is darker than a very pale orange, the aggregate must be washed. As I explained earlier, contaminated sand cannot be washed.

Buying aggregate

Try to purchase all materials by cubic measures, either cubic feet or cubic yards (usually cubic yards). In some areas, aggregates are still sold by weight, which is a fine way for the buyer to get ripped off. Water may add many tons to the weight of a load of sand or gravel, a tactic that is used all too often. You'll occasionally see gravel trucks driving down the road with water streaming from the bed. You know the aggregate in that truck has been sold by weight. Even when the seller is honest, changes in daily rainfall and general humidity mean great changes in the weight of the materials.

CONCRETE MIXTURES

The three methods of determining mixture proportions for concrete are book, trial, and absolute volume. In most cases, the first two must be combined because the book method requires adjustment after field testing is carried out. The absolute-volume method requires a *slump test*, a reasonably simple way for the novice to tell whether or not the mixture is within needed limits. Volume methods are most often used in home applications.

You must know the qualities of the concrete needed for a particular job, and then you mix to suit those qualities. For our purposes, the usual maximum slump is 6 inches, with a minimum of 3 inches, if the footings are to be reinforced (with steel bars). For nonreinforced footings, the maximum allowable slump is 4 inches (TABLE 3-1).

Slump test

To do a slump test, you need a *slump cone*, which you'll probably have to make yourself. The cone should be made of 16-gauge galvanized metal.

Table 3-1 Recommended Slumps

	Slump (inches)	
Type of construction	*Maximum*	*Minimum*
Reinforced foundation walls and footings	6	3
Unreinforced footings, caissons, and substructure walls	4	1
Reinforced slabs, beams, and walls	6	3
Building columns	6	4
Pavements	3	1
Heavy mass construction	3	1
Bridge decks	4	3
Sidewalk, driveway, and slabs on ground	6	3

The final product needs to be a foot high, with an 8-inch-diameter base and an open 4-inch-diameter top. You also need a 2-foot-long, smooth, pointed steel bar as a tamper. The cone can be made with tin snips, an electric drill, and a pop rivet gun.

Take samples for the slump test from the batch you're mixing as soon as the final wet mix is completed. After wetting the cone well, place a dampened flat board under it. Fill the cone in three layers, making each as close as possible to one third the cone's volume. As you pour, move the scoop or shovel around the edge of the cone instead of just dumping the concrete. You'll get a more symmetrical layer. Using the steel bar, rod in each layer immediately after placing it in the cone (FIG. 3-2). Try to move your strokes so as to mix as evenly as possible. Use 25 strokes per layer. Penetrate the new layer to the one below (hit the bottom board on the first layer). Once the cone is filled a bit over its top, strike off the excess with a straightedge, and gently lift the cone straight up. Measure the slump, using the cone as a guide (FIG. 3-3).

A final check of the slump mix will help show its workability and cohesiveness. Gently tap the side of the slumped mix with the tamping rod. If the mix is going to be easily workable, with good cohesiveness, it will merely slump a little bit lower. If, instead, it crumbles, the mix contains too much sand; if it separates, the mix contains too little sand.

Workability

Workability is an important factor with concrete, because a properly workable mix fills all form spaces completely. Ideally, when working out a cement-water ratio, only enough water is used to start hydration. A compromise is needed, since the resulting mix is too stiff to use in most applications. The slump test determines workability. The more slump, the greater the workability. If you have fairly complex forms, where a lot of flow is needed in a small area, go to slightly more slump (within allowable limits).

3-2   Rod in each layer in the slump cone through to the previous layer.

3-3   After removing the cone, measure the height of the slump and compare it with the height of the cone to determine the slump level of your mixture.

The problem of too much or too little sand is fixed by adding more cement or more sand, respectively. Extra water may also be used, but if you add extra water to the concrete to increase workability, you must also add extra cement to maintain the cement-water ratio.

As a rule, adding fine aggregate to a batch will make a stiffer mix, while adding coarse aggregate will loosen the mix.

MIXING CEMENT

Cement comes in 94-pound bags with a volume of just about 1 cubic foot. All portions of the mix are figured from that bag of cement. For home use, most mixes will use 1 part cement to 2 parts sand and 3 parts aggregate under 1½ inches. All measuring is done by volume, not by weight. For footings and walls where abrasion resistance isn't needed, proportions of 1 part cement, 2 parts sand, and 4 parts aggregates over 1½ inches may be used.

Water is an important part of the concrete mix and may cause some problems. For most do-it-yourself uses, extra care to get exact cement-water ratios is beyond our needs, as well as beyond our capabilities. Use a slump test and a tap test, and adjust as needed. Even using as much as 7 gallons of water per bag of cement will result in concrete strong enough for almost all home purposes.

For example, using 7 gallons of water to a bag of cement will give you concrete with compressive strength near 3,000 pounds per square inch, after a 28-day cure. No matter what you do to weaken or strengthen concrete, it will have low *tensile strength* (resistance to twisting forces). Low tensile strength—not much over 600 pounds per square inch—of concrete is the reason it cracks.

The dry mix must be complete. That is, sand, coarse aggregates, and cement must be thoroughly and completely mixed with one another before any water is added to the mix.

ESTIMATING AMOUNTS

The biggest problem with figuring amounts of concrete needed to fill forms is that most of the figuring must be done in inches, and then converted to cubic feet, or, preferably, cubic yards. For example, a usual footing for 8-inch block is 16 inches wide (footings are normally made twice as wide as what they support). If the footing is 12 inches deep and 20 feet (240 inches) long, you must determine the volume of that footing in cubic inches before it can be made useful. Thus,

$$16 \text{ in.} \times 12 \text{ in.} \times 240 \text{ in.} = 46,080 \text{ in.}^3$$

Reduce to cubic feet:

$$\frac{46,080 \text{ in.}^3}{1,728 \text{ in.}^3/\text{ft}^3} = 26.666 \text{ ft.}^3$$

A cubic yard contains 27 cubic feet, so you get an easy result here—a single cubic yard.

You must allow for a certain amount of waste when working with concrete. A percentage must be added for material because the bottom of the footing may not be perfectly flat, another amount sticks to the container, some spills over the sides of the wheelbarrow, and so on. If your original figure comes out under 5 cubic yards, add 15% to your total. For anything over 5 yards, add 10% for your waste allowance.

Ready-mix concrete generally comes in smaller sacks than regular concrete, so, although it's not practical for large brick masonry jobs, it's a super break for smaller projects. Such mixes used for large jobs raise costs far higher than materials you mix yourself, and use in concrete jobs is often ridiculously costly. Even delivered, ready-to-pour premix is far cheaper at today's prices.

Water mix is crucial with bagged mixes. If you use too much water, odds are that you will not have sand or cement on hand to correct things. Add water very slowly, starting from about half what you would normally estimate for such an amount of concrete or mortar. Most bagged mixes need under a gallon per bag, so begin with a couple of quarts (FIG. 3-4).

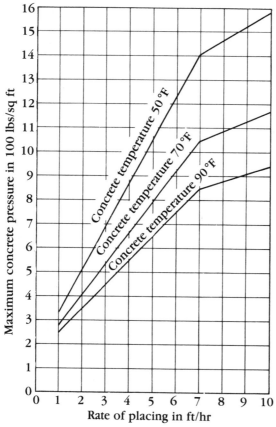

3-4 This graph shows the maximum amount of concrete to be placed per hour at specified temperatures. Use the table if you are planning to pour several feet of concrete.

FORMS

Occasionally, a footing may be poured directly in a neatly cut trench or hole in the ground, but usually some type of form is needed. Depending on complexity, the cost of forms for concrete work can be as much as a third of the total cost of the project (for concrete work, not for brickwork). It pays to design and build forms carefully. Sloppy or weak forms can result in inadequate bases for later brickwork. Expanses of concrete 16 feet long, 4 inches wide, and 2 feet high cannot be contained in forms made of 3/4-inch plywood, with anchors extending to the sides of the trench every couple of feet along the length. A badly bowed foundation wall is the best you can hope for in this situation. Frequently, such forms completely collapse in spots, forcing the addition of more concrete to fill the trench, which adds to cost but not to strength or appearance.

Most forms are for slabs, footings, or the occasional foundation wall to support brickwork. When it isn't possible to use the original trench, the form will usually be of wood. Metal forms that can be used many times are too expensive for one-time use around the home, but you might be able to rent one. Often, lumber used for building wooden forms can be used later in the job as sheathing or similar rough work where the surface doesn't matter or will be covered by siding or shingles.

Form lumber, oddly enough, is best made from green or only partially dried lumber. Kiln-dried lumber tends to absorb too much water from the concrete mix, causing the lumber to swell and, possibly, buckle or bulge. If you use green lumber, keep it wet until the concrete is poured so the drying wood doesn't shrink and distort the forms. For footing and most foundation work, rough-cut lumber (unplaned) is fine because the surfaces will not be seen later, so a coarse texture on the concrete is no problem. Lumber used to make forms for pieces or places that will be seen later should have at least the side facing the concrete planed.

Plywood used for forms must be made with waterproof glue, so choose one of the exterior grades. Form-grade plywood is also available, but in most cases CDX plywood at least 5/8-inch thick will suit the purpose and save money. Obviously, the larger your form, the thicker the lumber must be and the more closely the braces must be arranged.

Form design means building in enough strength to hold the concrete until it has hardened. Three variables affect the strength needed in your forms. The mixer output is important because a mixer that dumps a lot of concrete at one time builds up a greater pressure and needs a stronger form. The area to be enclosed in the form determines the total weight of the concrete to be dumped. The ambient temperature determines the time the concrete will take to set up, which in turn determines how long the form must remain durable. At about 70°F, concrete takes its initial set in 90 minutes or so. Higher temperatures give a slightly faster set, and colder weather results in a slower set.

When you use a hand- or motor-driven small mixer, you need to know the mixer yield in cubic feet and the time needed to prepare each batch. The following formula provides the mixer output figure:

$$\frac{\text{mixer yield (ft}^3)}{\text{batch time (min)}} \times \frac{60 \text{ min}}{1 \text{ hr}} = \text{mixer output (ft}^3/\text{hr})$$

The area of the form is found by multiplying the length times the width. Check a nearby outdoor thermometer for the local temperature. To get the rate of placement per hour, divide the mixer output in cubic feet by the plan area in square feet. Then, using FIG. 3-4, enter the rate of placement at the proper place on the chart and draw a vertical line to intersect the temperature line that is closest to the actual temperature. Read horizontally across to the left to find your maximum concrete pressure.

Use the maximum concrete pressure figure to determine maximum stud spacing by entering the pressure on the bottom of the chart in FIG. 3-5. Draw a vertical line up the chart until you reach the type of sheathing you are going to use. Follow a horizontal line to the left to get maximum stud spacing for supports. If the answer lands on an odd number, such as 25, decrease the figure to the lower even number, in this case, 24 inches. This reduction increases your margin of safety, while giving you common, easy units to use.

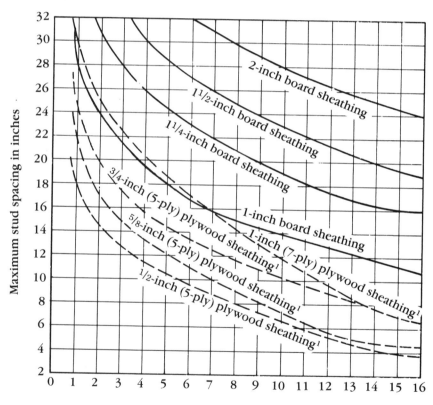

Maximum concrete pressure in 100 lbs/ft²

I Sanded face grain parallel to span

3-5 This chart shows the maximum pressure of concrete that various types of sheathing can withstand at different stud spacings. The maximum allowable stud spacing is 32 inches.

The next equation determines the uniform load on each stud:

$$\text{Maximum concrete pressure (lbs/ft}^2) \times \text{stud spacing (ft)}$$
$$= \text{uniform load on stud (lbs/ft)}$$

Enter this number on the bottom line of the chart in FIG. 3-6, and draw a vertical line until it cuts across the correct stud size curve. Read horizontally to get the correct maximum *wale* spacing, which is again rounded down to an even number if necessary.

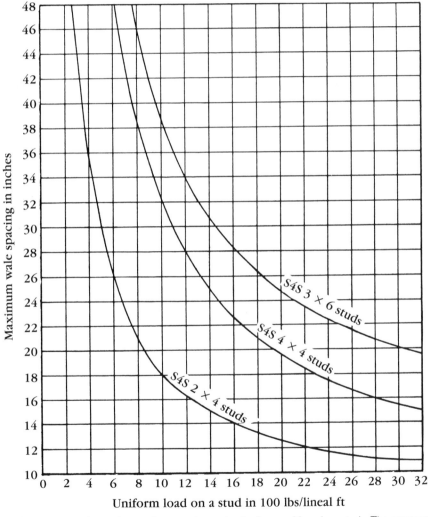

3-6 This chart shows the maximum wale spacing for forms with various studs. The greatest allowable spacing is 48 inches.

For larger wale areas, tie wires may be needed. Their maximum spacing must also be determined. The uniform load on a wale is needed to figure tie wire spacing. The formula is:

Maximum concrete pressure (lbs/ft²) × wale spacing (ft)
= uniform load on a wale (lbs/ft)

Use FIG. 3-7 to get the maximum spacing. Again, numbers are rounded down if needed. Tie wire strength is also a factor here. Table 3-2 gives minimum breaking loads for types of tie wire where strength is not known. To figure tie wire spacing:

$$\frac{\text{Breaking load (lbs)} \times 12 \text{ (in/ft)}}{\text{uniform load on wale (lbs/ft)}} = \text{spacing (in)}$$

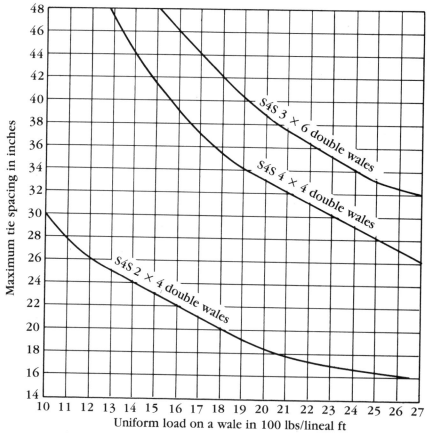

3-7 Use this chart to determine the maximum allowable tie spacing for your wall. Maximum allowable tie spacing is 48 inches.

Table 3-2 Breaking Load of Wire

Steel wire	
Size of wire (gauge number)	*Minimum breaking load double strand (pounds)*
8	1,700
9	1,420
10	1,170
11	930
Barbed wire	
Size of each wire (gauge number)	*Minimum breaking load (pounds)*
12 1/2	950
13	660
13 1/2	950
14	650
15 1/2	850

If the tie wire spacing is shorter than the maximum stud spacing, reduce the stud spacing to suit. If maximum tie wire spacing is greater than the stud spacing, tie at the intersections of studs and wales.

When all the design details are complete, actual form construction is fairly simple. Make any excavation needed, always going below the local frost depth for footings and foundation walls. Nail sizes will vary depending on the materials sizes, but make certain you get good penetration for holding power. For basic brickwork, directly on a footing, keying the footing (laying in a beveled 2 × 4 to form a key) is not needed. But if a concrete wall will be built on the footing, and later faced in brick, keying is good for increased strength. Figures 3-8 through 3-18 illustrate construction of various types of forms.

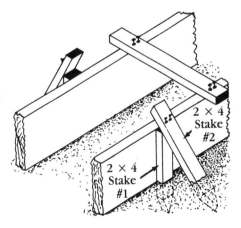

3-8 In this typical wall footing form, stake #1 holds the form to elevation while stake #2 holds it in line.

2 × 4 Stake #2

2 × 4 Stake #1

Spreader nailed to from sides

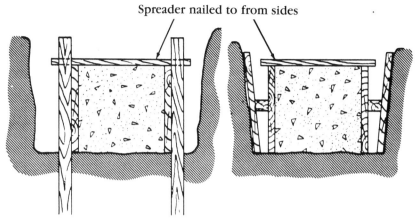

3-9   Spreaders are used to brace footing forms.

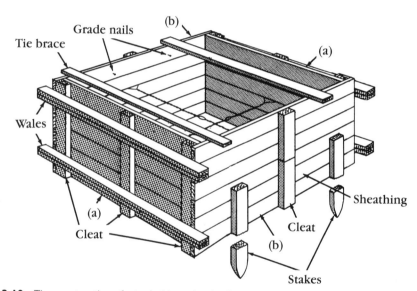

3-10   The construction of a typical large footing form includes reinforcing bars and braces.

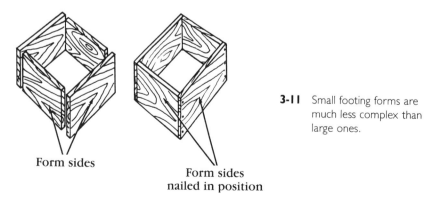

3-11   Small footing forms are much less complex than large ones.

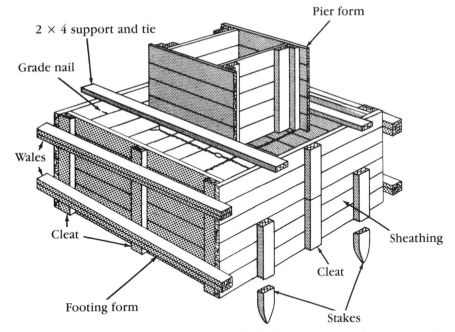

3-12 If you must place a pier form on top of a footing form, support the pier form with 2 × 4s so that it doesn't interfere with the placement of concrete in the lower form.

3-13 Column forms are supported by a series of yokes.

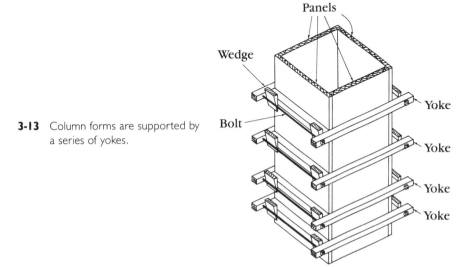

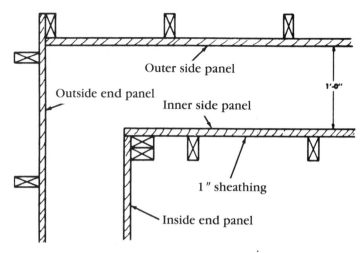

3-14 Join wall form panels at corners as illustrated.

3-15 Use doubleheaded nails and wood blocks to join sheathing panels in a line.

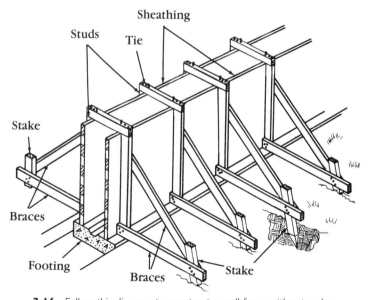

3-16 Follow this diagram to construct a wall form without wales.

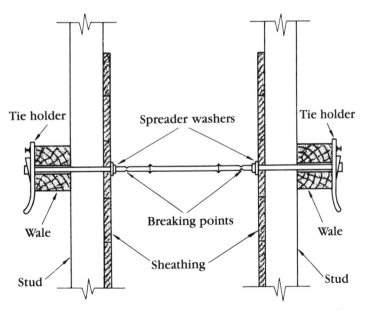

3-17 This diagram shows the placement of wales on a wall form.

3-18 Snap ties such as this one are manufactured to replace wire ties and wooden spreaders in form construction.

Oil the 2 × 4 before inserting it in the concrete at the top of the footing. Form panels will have less concrete stick to them if they're also oiled before the pour is made, but a coat of paint will do almost as good a job and might make the lumber more suitable for later use as roof or wall sheathing.

POURING FOOTINGS

Excavation for footings must be no less than specified by your local building codes. Most often you must dig at least to the frost level. If the earth is disturbed, soft, or easily moved, you may have to go deeper to reach firm ground. One other solution for footings on soft or wet ground is to increase the width of the footing so it floats its load over a wider area. This technique helps prevent shifting and cracking of the concrete and any structure built on the footing. Before making your pour, moisten the earth at the bottom of the forms.

Deposit the concrete in horizontal layers as evenly as possible. Layers must be no less than 6 inches deep, with each succeeding layer poured before the layer ahead has had time to take its initial set.

Use a *screed*—a straight-edged board—to strike off excess concrete at the tops of the forms (FIG. 3-19).

3-19 Attach handles to a 2 × 6 or 2 × 4 timber to make a screed. Use heavier timber for wider forms. Two people screed the top of the poured concrete.

Once the concrete is in place, curing begins. Concrete cures by a process known as hydration. To get a good cure, concrete must be kept moist. Two methods are used. One prevents the loss of water from the concrete after it is poured. The second adds water to the surface after pouring.

The best curing method is to inhibit evaporation by laying plastic sheeting over the poured concrete. A 7-day minimum cure is best. A lot of figures use 28-day cure strengths, but that's a long time to hold up any project. Most concrete mixtures reach a large percentage of their 28-day strength within 7 days of being poured. Leave forms in place for the entire curing period, both as a support for the uncured concrete and as moisture retainers. If the weather is hot and dry, spray the forms daily to cut down on rapid water loss.

MORTAR

Without good mortar, no amount of work will give you a strong, attractive, durable brick or block wall. Good mortar provides a strong bond between the masonry units while minimizing water seepage into the joints. Bond strength is affected by several factors, including the type and quantity of cement used, the surface texture of the mortar bedding areas on the masonry units (the smoother the units, the less surface area to which the mortar can bond), the plasticity of the mortar, and the water retention of the mortar. Craftsmanship in laying the masonry units is of great importance in forming the bond. Because most masonry walls suffer their worst water leakage at the mortar joints, good mortar combined with good joint tooling are essential to the construction of a durable wall.

Mortar in its proper form is plastic enough to be worked with a trowel without segregating. Segregating is caused by too much sand in the mixture. Also essential is using only good, clean sand. Some masons insist on using what is known as sharp sand, but smooth sand forms just as good a bond, so don't spend extra time looking for sharp sand if it's hard to find. You obtain the proper plasticity, or workability, through the use of top-quality materials in proper proportions. Add enough water to give the correct consistency, but not so much as to give a slushy mixture that will run out on the faces of the bricks.

Concrete block is not wetted before application of mortar, but most types of brick must be. To wet bricks, direct a stream of water onto them until water runs off the surfaces. Allow the bricks to surface dry before bedding them in mortar.

Two types of cement are used to produce mortar. Masonry cement is often difficult to find, while Portland cement is readily available in most areas. No matter what type of cement is used, the durability of the mortar is controlled by the proportions of the materials. Mortar for ordinary service uses 1 measure of either masonry or Portland cement. With Portland cement, add $1/2$ to $1^1/4$ measures of hydrated lime and $4^1/2$ to 6 measures of masonry sand in a damp, loose condition. The masonry cement requires no lime and only $2^1/4$ to 3 measures of sand. As always, make all measurements by volume, not by weight. For masonry joints that must endure severe conditions, such as violent winds or many freeze-thaw cycles, use 1 part masonry cement, 1 part Portland cement, and 4½ to 6 parts sand. Or use 1 part Portland cement, a ¼ measure of hydrated lime, and no more than 3 parts sand.

Mortar types are designated M, S, N, and O. While not all of these are likely to be needed around a home or farm, in a few cases, one or the other would improve durability over standard mortars.

Type M mortar needs 1 part Portland cement, ¼ part hydrated lime, and 3 parts sand. It is a general-use mortar that is particularly suitable for below-grade use and use in contact with the ground. It is most often used for retaining walls.

Type S mortar takes 1 part Portland cement, ½ part hydrated lime, and 4½ parts sand. Type S is a general-use mortar especially good where high resistance to lateral forces (high winds) is needed.

Type N mortar takes 1 part Portland cement, 1 part hydrated lime, and 6 parts sand. Type N is designed to work best where exterior conditions are liable to be nasty, with a lot of salt flying through the air—coastal and beach area uses.

Type O mortar uses 1 part Portland cement, 2 parts hydrated lime, and 9 parts of sand. This is another general-use mortar, fairly light duty, where bearing walls don't get pressures over 10 pounds per square inch. It is very resistant to moisture and freezing.

Mortar is always mixed in much smaller amounts than concrete. You can buy, build, or rent a mortar box (FIGS. 3-20 and 3-21). You may also use a wheelbarrow that is fairly leakproof. One method of mixing is to measure all dry ingredients and mix them thoroughly before you add any water. Use a spade to pull dry mortar from the corners of the box when you are doing the final mixing. You can use your hoe for this chore if a spade is not handy.

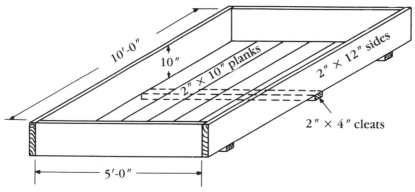

3-20   You can make your own mortar box or buy one.

Some masons prefer to start the mix with half the necessary water. Then they add the mortar mix and half the sand before adding more water and sand.

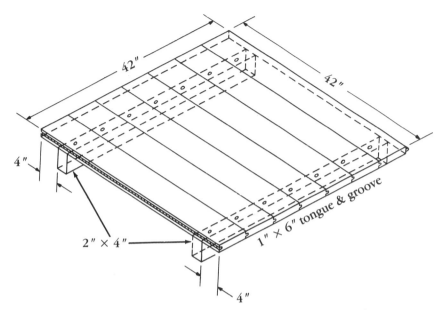

3-21 A mortar board is another useful tool in masonry work.

You can retemper mortar that has stiffened through evaporation by mixing in a small amount of extra water. Do not use mortar which has partially set: it will ruin the bond. If mortar has set for two hours in 80 °F temperatures, discard it. If the temperature is below 80 °F and the mix is more than three hours old, discard it.

Because the bond formed by the mortar joint is of such great importance to the finished brick or concrete block masonry, do not indulge in false economy. Discarding half a box of mortar is cheaper than having a weak bond at a crucial point in the project. If you have any doubts at all about whether you can retemper partially set mortar, discard it and mix a new batch.

Chapter **4**

Concrete blocks

While this book deals with brick masonry, information on concrete and concrete blocks is also necessary because in most construction, brickwork requires some form of backing to provide an attractive wall, patio, walkway, or staircase at a reasonable cost.

BLOCK SIZE

The most obvious and immediate difference between bricks and blocks is size. While many sizes of concrete blocks are available, the standard nominal size is 8 × 8 × 16 inches. A hollow-core load-bearing block of standard size will weigh from 40 to 50 pounds. Concrete blocks do not provide an attractive final finish for residential construction work. It usually is covered with bricks or other types of veneer.

Figure 4-1 shows typical sizes and styles of concrete blocks. The variety is needed for the wide range of shapes of building projects common in construction. When possible, use blocks specifically designed for the purpose at hand rather than try to cut blocks to unusual shapes or sizes. You must do modular planning to determine the number of half blocks and lintels your project requires.

FOOTINGS

When you start a wall, your footings must be at least twice as wide as the wall that will rest on them. If the soil underneath does not bear loads well, they should be even wider. Footings should be below frost level, and you must provide proper drainage.

Concrete blocks are laid in much the same manner as bricks, with the basic exception of running mortar beds on the blocks in two strips outside the block cores. Butter the ends of the blocks along the raised outside edges (FIG. 4-2). Block units are large enough to check with a level

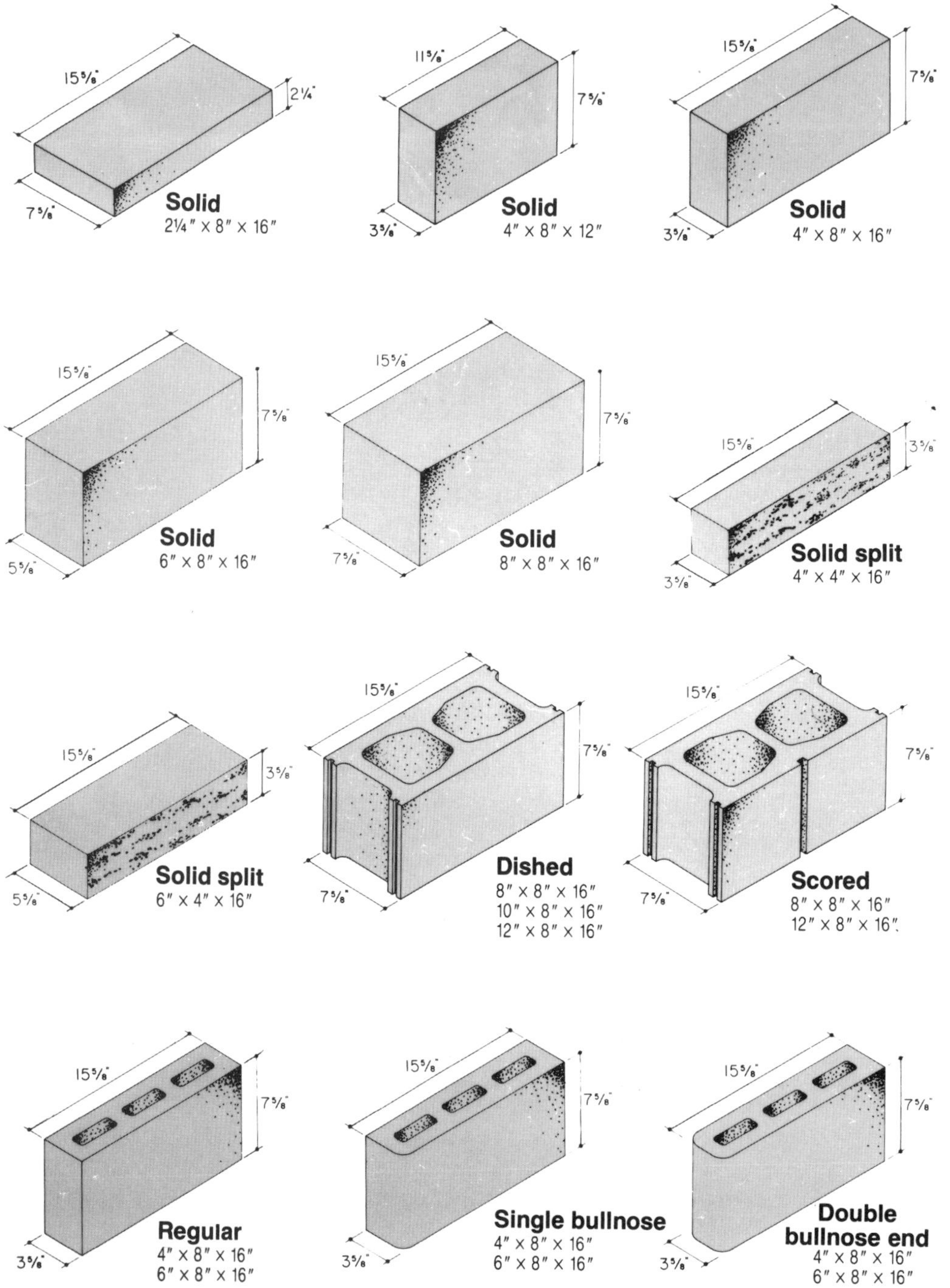

Solid
2¼" × 8" × 16"
15⅝"
7⅝"
2¼"

Solid
4" × 8" × 12"
11⅝"
7⅝"
3⅝"

Solid
4" × 8" × 16"
15⅝"
7⅝"
3⅝"

Solid
6" × 8" × 16"
15⅝"
7⅝"
5⅝"

Solid
8" × 8" × 16"
15⅝"
7⅝"
7⅝"

Solid split
4" × 4" × 16"
15⅝"
3⅝"
3⅝"

Solid split
6" × 4" × 16"
15⅝"
3⅝"
5⅝"

Dished
8" × 8" × 16"
10" × 8" × 16"
12" × 8" × 16"
15⅝"
7⅝"
7⅝"

Scored
8" × 8" × 16"
12" × 8" × 16"
15⅝"
7⅝"
7⅝"

Regular
4" × 8" × 16"
6" × 8" × 16"
15⅝"
7⅝"
3⅝"

Single bullnose
4" × 8" × 16"
6" × 8" × 16"
15⅝"
7⅝"
3⅝"

Double bullnose end
4" × 8" × 16"
6" × 8" × 16"
15⅝"
7⅝"
3⅝"

4-1   Concrete blocks, like bricks, come in a variety of sizes and shapes designed to meet the wide-ranging needs of builders. General Shale Products Corp.

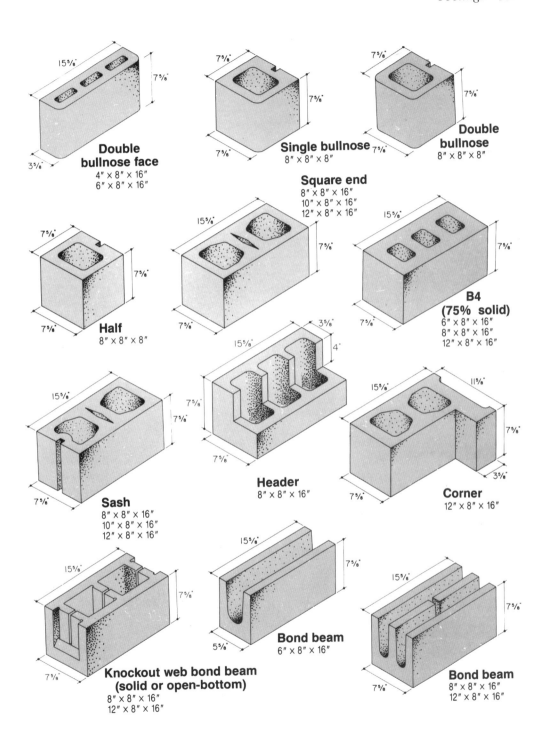

Double bullnose face
4" × 8" × 16"
6" × 8" × 16"

Single bullnose
8" × 8" × 8"

Double bullnose
8" × 8" × 8"

Square end
8" × 8" × 16"
10" × 8" × 16"
12" × 8" × 16"

Half
8" × 8" × 8"

B4 (75% solid)
6" × 8" × 16"
8" × 8" × 16"
12" × 8" × 16"

Sash
8" × 8" × 16"
10" × 8" × 16"
12" × 8" × 16"

Header
8" × 8" × 16"

Corner
12" × 8" × 16"

Knockout web bond beam (solid or open-bottom)
8" × 8" × 16"
12" × 8" × 16"

Bond beam
6" × 8" × 16"

Bond beam
8" × 8" × 16"
12" × 8" × 16"

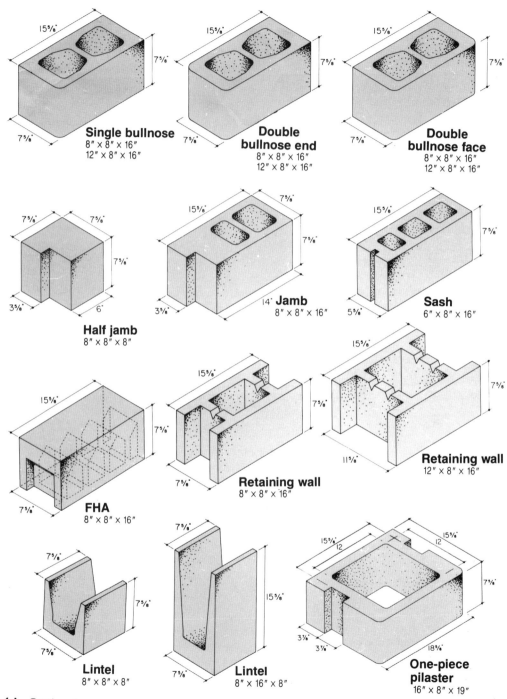

Single bullnose
8″ × 8″ × 16″
12″ × 8″ × 16″

Double bullnose end
8″ × 8″ × 16″
12″ × 8″ × 16″

Double bullnose face
8″ × 8″ × 16″
12″ × 8″ × 16″

Half jamb
8″ × 8″ × 8″

Jamb
8″ × 8″ × 16″

Sash
6″ × 8″ × 16″

FHA
8″ × 8″ × 16″

Retaining wall
8″ × 8″ × 16″

Retaining wall
12″ × 8″ × 16″

Lintel
8″ × 8″ × 8″

Lintel
8″ × 16″ × 8″

One-piece pilaster
16″ × 8″ × 19″

4-1 Continued.

4-2 Blocks, like bricks, are laid in bonded courses. Butter the end of each block along the outside edges. Note that the second course of blocks is laid so that the midpoint lies above the joints of the blocks below.

after every two blocks are laid. You should also use the level to check the blocks in all appropriate directions. Blocks should be level along the course line, from side to side across the course line, and vertically plumb (FIG. 4-3).

Continue to use the guide line (FIGS. 4-4 and 4-5) as you work upward and along each course. Position the blocks so that they are as close as possible to the line without actually touching it.

You also can use a *story pole*. A story pole is a pole or timber (a 2 × 4 works well) marked to show the height of each course. Compare the final block on each end of the course with the marked ideal height on the story pole. You can also check mid-course heights if you wish.

TOOLING JOINTS

Joint tooling is done after a wall section is laid. Press your thumb against the joint mortar, and if the mortar will take a print, it's time to tool the joint. For concrete block, tool the horizontal joints first, using only concave or V-joint tools. Make sure the jointing tool, as with brick, is a bit wider than the joint being worked.

CONTROL JOINTS

In long concrete block walls, control joints may be needed. As time passes, movement in the wall might occur. Control joints permit that

4-3   Use a level as well as a guide line to make sure your courses stay properly aligned. The bubble on the level should be centered, and the block should come to within a fraction of an inch of touching the guide line.

4-4   Spread mortar along the outside edges of the blocks and along the center.

4-5 Lay a block in place with its center over the joint in the course below.

movement, within limits, and cut down on checking of the wall. Half blocks are used to form a continuous vertical joint, which is filled with mortar. As soon as the mortar sets, rake it out to a depth of about $3/4$ inch. The resulting gap is caulked with a top grade silicone caulk.

From this point on, laying of concrete block strongly resembles the laying of brick. Figures 4-6 through 4-9 illustrate some of the steps involved. Needed changes in method should be obvious as you go along.

Precast lintels over doors are installed as the wall goes up, as are those over the windows, but the precast sills used under windows are often put in place after other construction is finished. Sills and lintels are available in sizes to fit standard doors and windows (FIG. 4-10).

CONCRETE COATINGS

Concrete is an extremely popular building material for a number of reasons: it is durable, easy to clean, fire-resistant, and inexpensive to maintain. The fact that concrete is plastic when properly mixed means it can be readily shaped into many forms, from floors to walls to walks and drives. Once those shapes become solid, concrete poses a few finishing problems that other building materials do not.

On floors, dusting is almost always a problem until the concrete is coated. Walls may seep or leak and refuse to accept coatings, while *efflorescence* may create problems with keeping the finish on a concrete surface, though it is otherwise harmless.

4-6 Butter the edges of the next blocks to be laid.

4-7 Lay the buttered block as shown.

4-8 Shove the new block against the previous block to compact the mortar.

4-9 Cut away excess mortar and return it to the mortar board for future use.

Concrete walls are permeable until they are sealed: water penetrates and flows through the walls, creating moisture problems. Much of this can be relieved by directing moisture flow away from the concrete walls with proper grading and good gutter systems, but masonry walls still need coatings to become impermeable to moisture.

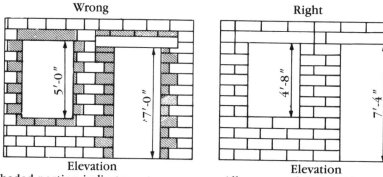

4-10 Plan wall openings so that you do not need to cut bricks or blocks to install windows and doors. The shaded areas represent cut masonry.

As with finishes on other materials, surface preparation is of great importance: loose mortar, dirt, and other foreign substances must be removed. A wire brush works well for most matter, and grease can be removed with detergents and washing. Efflorescence creates some special needs.

All masonry surfaces are subject to efflorescence, the leaching out of water-soluble salts that make up a fraction of a percent of the concrete or masonry mixture. Cold weather tends to speed the migration of salts to the surface. Over time, the deposits usually clear as the salts leach out of the materials, but that can take years. Efflorescence shows up as a white, chalky substance on the surface of the concrete.

Part of the elimination of efflorescence is taken care of by using washed aggregate and clean mixing water and tools. Later problems can be prevented by stopping the passage of water through concrete, something that many coatings do well, others less well. In some instances, efflorescence can lead to *spalling* (chipping and flaking) of concrete surfaces if an improper surface treatment is used.

Removing efflorescence is the first step in getting the concrete coated properly. This job traditionally has been done with muriatic acid. Most people are happier not having to deal with strong acids, so a substance such as UGL's Drylok Etch is a better alternative for removing efflorescence and cleaning mortar stains from brick and ceramic tile.

Whether you use Drylok Etch or muriatic acid, you must wear proper eye protection, along with rubber gloves and a long-sleeved work shirt. Always follow cautionary directions on the packaging of such materials.

Any patching should be done with the appropriate material: for very wet areas, use a hydraulic cement such as Drylok Fast Plug, which will fill holes even with water running through them—though it works best when the water flow is stopped first.

Wall coatings can then be selected and applied. Clear coatings, such as Drylok Clear Masonry Sealer and Drylok Clear Masonry Acrylic Treatment, in standard and acrylic (water-soluble) formulations are available and do a fine job of coating surfaces to prevent dusting and stopping water penetration in walls. Available in waterborne and petroleum-distillate acrylic versions, clear sealers penetrate concrete and other masonry surfaces to prevent or retard dusting, staining, spalling, and general surface deterioration. Acrylic versions are not suitable for finish coats on floors because they are not made to withstand abrasion, but they do make excellent primer coats for floor paint.

Opaque wall coatings should include a special grade of Portland cement and an acrylic resin compound that will, when dry, resist water pressure of four pounds per square foot. Drylok Masonry Waterproofer meets those specifications, withstanding the equivalent pressure of a 9-foot column of water. The material can be brushed, rolled, or sprayed on the wall. Each gallon covers 75 to 100 square feet. If the wall is damp, first brush a coat on the lower third of the wall and let dry 24 hours. Once the first coat stops most of the seepage, a second coat can be applied over the entire wall. If some seepage still remains, recoating any seeping areas after several days will usually solve the problem.

Do not brush too actively, as that spreads the waterproofer too thin, but make sure that pores are fully covered. If you use less than a gallon for each 100 square feet, you will need to recoat the area, as the material is spread too thin to waterproof properly. For greater economy where waterproofing is not needed, dry-cement paints work well.

Dry-cement paints are applied over surfaces in much the same manner as sealants, after being mixed with water. They are generally brushed on, using a heavy brush in a scrubbing motion, with no overlap. Such paints can be used readily over old finishes. Water protection is not as great, and the material goes on best over a well-dampened surface. (Drylok Double Duty Sealer is a white, dry sealer that provides an above- and below-grade sealer, in economical form, that goes on in the same manner as cement paint, but provides a seal for any masonry surface.) Make sure surface water is thoroughly absorbed before painting.

After the wall is dampened, if drying occurs in a patchy manner, the wall is not sufficiently wet. Wet surfaces until water is absorbed uniformly. Keep the walls damp as you paint.

Floors present a special problem, because not only must the coating adhere to concrete, but it must resist abrasive wear as well. Again, cleanliness of the surface to be painted is essential: As much dust as possible needs to be removed before the paint, or primer-sealer, is laid on the surface.

Dusting is often a problem of massive proportions on uncoated concrete floors. The floor seems as dusty after sweeping and vacuuming as before. It is, of course, not the only cleanliness problem reduced or eliminated by painting, for a good paint also will not allow grease or other prime to penetrate and become a permanent part of the floor.

Make sure the floor to be painted is free of all grease, wax, soap, or any oily film from sweeping compounds before getting ready to paint.

Where dusting is a major problem, cut masonry sealer with an equal amount of mineral spirits and prime the floor before painting, giving the appropriate drying time (at least six hours). The concrete floor paint may be brushed or rolled on. For previously painted surfaces, break any gloss on the remaining paint, and spot-prime bare sections with masonry sealer. Use at least two coats, working the first coat in with a brush, if possible, and rolling or brushing on the second coat.

All concrete coatings must be applied when the temperature is above 45 degrees. Products come in light tints for walls, and numerous other tints for floors; the light-colored materials may be enhanced with alkali-proof universal tinting colors.

Chapter **5**

Reinforcing brick masonry

*T*he major drawback of mortared masonry construction is its lack of resistance to tension. Reinforcing brick, and block, masonry to create greater resistance to tension can be accomplished in several ways. Because the tensile strength of a brick wall is quite low when compared to its compressive strength, reinforcement is often desirable. The chapters on brick cavity walls (chapter 6) and veneers (chapter 11) show how brick ties increase single wythe strength and tie two wythes into a more cohesive unit. Other methods of reinforcement can be added or used alone. The most attractive, and arguably the best, of these is the use of *pilasters* in brick walls over 3 feet tall.

PILASTERS

Pilasters (columns) connected to the wall at proper intervals add a great deal of strength, making the wall much more resistant to twisting forces. Usually, such pilasters are given concrete footings, set below frost level, and the pilasters have two or more reinforcing bars run vertically to increase their own strength.

Pilasters are placed at regular intervals, determined by expected wind loadings and wall height. A 5-foot wall under moderate wind load conditions might need a pilaster only every dozen feet or so, while high winds, or a taller wall, will force closer spacing of pilasters, possibly as close as every 6 feet.

When no pilasters are used to reinforce a wall, reinforcement steel bars (FIG. 5-1) can be placed in the horizontal mortar joints. Steel might also be used in some vertical joints, depending on the bond style used. Where bond styles use staggered vertical joints in a single wythe wall, reinforcing steel cannot be placed in those joints. In such cases, pilasters must be used, but may be placed at quite wide intervals because the hori-

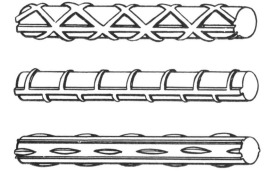

5-1 You can use steel reinforcing bars to increase the tensile strength of concrete work. You will need to make mortar joints at least 1/8 inch thicker than the diameter of the steel bar.

zontal bars help tie the wall together. Metal ties are used to hook the pilasters into the wall if the brickwork doesn't overlap.

Bricks used in reinforced brick masonry must have a compressive strength of at least 2,500 pounds per square inch. Type N mortar is used because of its strength. Metal used as reinforcement is a fairly soft grade because of the many sharp turns needed—malleable metal is easier to bend. Any wire used to tie bars together must be 18-gauge, soft-annealed.

The method of laying up brick for reinforced walls differs very little from standard bricklaying. A few considerations must be kept in mind: mortar joints must be 1/8 inch thicker than the steel used for reinforcement, so that at least 1/16 inch of mortar lies above and below the bar. If a large steel bar is used, you might have mortar joints as thick as 5/8 inch, a full 1/4 inch thicker than standard.

HORIZONTAL BARS

Lay horizontal bars in the mortar bed and shove them down until they're in the right position. At least 1/16 inch of mortar must support the bar. Add mortar over the bar and smooth it to get a bed that provides a joint of the correct thickness. Then lay the brick in this bed just as if the reinforcing bar weren't in place.

Z-shaped stirrups are used to tie in vertical joints, as FIG. 5-2 shows. As you can see, laying the stirrup leg under the horizontal bar requires a thicker than usual joint.

VERTICAL BARS

Vertical bars are placed in head joints (vertical joints), and are held in place by wooden templates that have been drilled for the correct bar spacing. The brick is then laid around the vertical bars. Parallel bars must be placed at a minimum of 1 1/2 times their diameters apart.

Reinforced masonry columns and walls are useful around the home and farm. When you're erecting a reinforced brick column, the steel bars need a covering of at least 1 1/2 inches of mortar. They can be held in place with 3/8-inch-diameter steel hoops or ties. Hoops are usually laid in the horizontal joints with a single tie to one vertical bar at each joint. The bars are placed inside the hoop, as shown in FIG. 5-3.

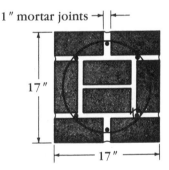

Stirrup is placed in vertical
joint between headers

Z-shaped stirrup

5-2 Vertical reinforcing, like this
Z-shaped stirrup, can add
to the strength and
endurance of masonry
work. Note the proper
points of horizontal
reinforcement indicated by
the dots above the lower
leg of the stirrup.

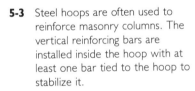

1″ mortar joints

17″

17″

5-3 Steel hoops are often used to
reinforce masonry columns. The
vertical reinforcing bars are
installed inside the hoop with at
least one bar tied to the hoop to
stabilize it.

Hoops are used at every course of brick. Once the footings are in,
with the steel rods in place, place a wooden template over the tops of the
bars. Slip the hoops over the bars first, and tie off one or two to keep
them from slipping down and interfering with bricklaying. Pull each
hoop down to its course, tie it to a vertical bar, and embed it in mortar. For
some types of columns, bats (half bricks) must be used in a mortar bed as
column center fillers. For others, use full bricks. Always fill any remaining
center column space with mortar, course by course as you lay the bricks.

For corner leads in walls, place the bars so 15 inches extend out over
the ends of the leads. Use the same bar size as for the rest of the wall.
Allow the horizontal bars in the wall to overlap the lead bars for that 15
inches (FIG. 5-4).

Reinforcing steel bars for brick masonry walls are the same type,
though usually smaller in diameter, as those used to reinforce concrete. A

Reinforcing bars with 15″ extension

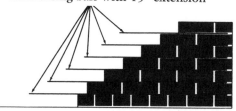

5-4 In laying corners, let the lead bars extend 15 inches past the lead bricks.

number on the end of each bar shows the bar's nominal diameter in eighths of an inch. Reinforcing steel sizes start at 3 and go to 18; brick masonry size is 3, and, on occasion, 4. Anything else forces the use of a joint that is too greatly oversized. Figure 5-5 illustrates the markings on steel reinforcing bars, and TABLE 5-1 gives specifications for the standard sizes.

Continuous line system—grade marks

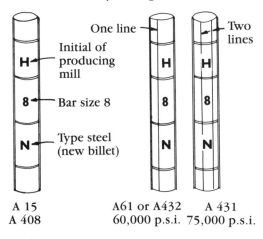

A 15
A 408

A61 or A432   A 431
60,000 p.s.i. 75,000 p.s.i.

5-5 The grade and size of steel reinforcing bars are indicated on the bars themselves by one of two systems.

Number system—grade marks

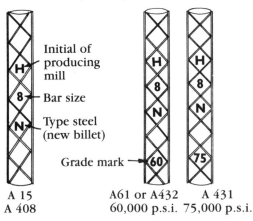

A 15
A 408

A61 or A432   A 431
60,000 p.s.i. 75,000 p.s.i.

Table 5-1 Standard Steel Reinforcing Bars

Bar designation No.*	Unit weight (Pound/feet)	Diameter (Inches)	Cross-sectional area (Square inches)	Perimeter (Inches)
3	.376	0.375	0.11	1.178
4	.668	0.500	0.20	1.571
5	1.043	0.625	0.31	1.963
6	1.502	0.750	0.44	2.356
7	2.044	0.875	0.60	2.749
8	2.670	1.000	0.79	3.142
9	3.400	1.128	1.00	3.544
10	4.303	1.270	1.27	3.990
11	5.313	1.410	1.56	4.430
14	7.65	1.693	2.25	5.32
18	13.60	2.257	4.00	7.09

*Bar numbers are based on the number of eighths of an inch included in the nominal diameter of the bars.

Reinforcing bars are made of ductile steel to allow the forming of corner stirrups. If you use the *jig* shown in FIG. 5-6, you can form your own stirrups.

Always remember to keep reinforcing steel free of grease, loose rust, and scale.

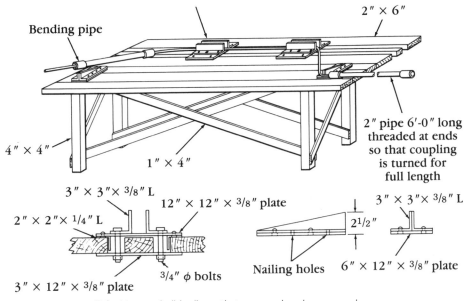

5-6 You can build a jig so that you can bend your own bars.

Chapter **6**

Special walls

Because this book is meant for the amateur bricklayer who will be most interested in projects around the house and yard, I won't go into elaborate work like arches and serpentine walls. These very complex types of work can be difficult even for the most experienced masons. In this chapter, I'll discuss cavity walls, rowlock walls, thin brick walls, beams, and doors and windows.

CAVITY WALLS

Solid brick walls are excellent as decorative and retaining walls, among other uses, but for heat retention and sound insulation, other types of walls are necessary. A solid brick wall would need to be at least 48 inches thick to achieve the same thermal insulation value as a standard frame wall. Fortunately, brick walls can be constructed in ways that cut down on heat loss.

Any wall allows some heat loss although modern insulations cut such losses to a minimum. The greatest heat losses usually result from the metal ties that hold the wythes of a hollow-cavity wall together. Some heat also escapes through the ties that hold brick veneer facing on the frame wall behind it, but insulation in the wall should reduce such losses to a negligible amount (FIG. 6-1).

It's a toss-up as to which type of brick wall is more useful, the brick cavity wall or the veneer wall. In most brick home construction today, the veneer wall reigns, but for other uses, cavity walls are excellent. They also work well in home construction, but tend to be more costly than veneer walls. A brick cavity wall is impervious to moisture penetration, even though the outer section, or wythe, may not be completely waterproof. Any water that does penetrate runs down the inside of the outer wythe and is directed to the outside of the wall's base by weep holes and flashing. All cavity walls have flashing installed along their bases with weep

6-1 If a brick wall is constructed properly, heat loss can be kept to a minimum. The greatest loss comes from the metal ties used to hold the wythes of a hollow cavity wall together.

holes every 2 feet on center. The flashing goes on top of the second course of the inside wythe and is bent down to go under the mortar bed of the outside wythe. Weep holes are placed directly over the flashing so any accumulated water has an easy flow path to the outside.

Walls with 3-inch-minimum cavities provide much better thermal insulation, alone, than a solid brick wall of the same total thickness. Adding water-resistant insulating material between the wythes increases the thermal-flow resistance even more. To ensure that water does not create problems, use glass fiber or granular or solid-foamed plastic insulation materials. The granular material must be a type that won't clog weep holes (possibly granular vermiculite or silicone-treated perlite). Rigid foam board insulation is great, and has a high R (thermal resistance) value per inch, but is fairly costly.

Cavity walls offer good insulation against sound transmission, too. Traditionally, two methods of preventing sound transmission have been effective: massive construction and discontinuous construction. Cavity walls use massive materials that are discontinuous. The sound of a hammer rap on the outer wythe will travel fairly rapidly through that wythe, but will meet dead air, which interferes with sound transmission. Insulation itself doesn't provide resistance to heat or sound transfer; lack of air movement does. Insulation provides pockets of dead or unmoving air, which transmit neither sound nor heat well.

Metal ties must be used to tie wythes together in cavity walls. On 2-foot centers, place the ties every sixth course, making sure the ties are galvanized metal or stainless steel (FIG. 6-2). Galvanized is more commonly used because stainless steel is expensive.

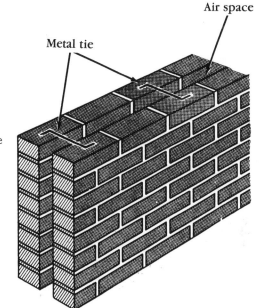

6-2 Galvanized metal ties are used to hold wythes together in cavity walls.

Mortar used for cavity walls is the same as for all brick walls, but Type S is preferable if winds in excess of 80 mph are expected. The best flashing is sheet aluminum; plastics sometimes fail, and replacing flashing in brick cavity walls is an expensive and extensive job. Start with the best, do it right, and prevent problems.

Bonds used to construct cavity walls are the same as for any type of brick construction, although common, running, and American bonds are the most widely used patterns. Where bricks are turned end on, use half-bricks (bats) to leave the cavity as open as possible.

Detailing in cavity wall construction is important since such walls are almost always part of a home. Bonding includes brick ties at least $3/16$ inch in diameter, with enough length for each end to have a 2-inch hook bent in. One tie must be used in every $4^1/2$ square feet of wall area, with ties no further apart than 24 inches horizontally and 36 inches vertically. Use ties within a foot of all openings, spacing them no further apart than 3 feet around the wall's perimeter.

Weep holes are also necessary. They must run above every strip of flashing, no further apart than 24 inches on center. If weep holes and flashing are not fashioned correctly, the interior wall might be always damp. All caps, coping, and lintels also must be flashed, with weep holes.

Windows and doors

Standard windows and doors can be easily set back, or forward, into cavity walls, but knowing the depth of the wall and ordering the units correctly is a better method. Recently, I replaced a door in a block basement wall. MW Windows of Rocky Mount, Virginia, made a special frame mount for the door to fit the 8-inch block exactly. The new unit worked much better than the earlier improvised model. Brick cavity walls tend to be even thicker, and a five-inch window or door unit lacks in aesthetics.

Many builders prefer to work with wood rather than vinyl for windows and doors. In some vinyl windows, the muntins separate from the frame under extreme summer heat. Strong arguments can be advanced for buying more expensive windows, because the extra cost will actually result in savings on fuel and cooling costs because double- and triple-glazed units provide superior resistance to loss of heating and cooling.

Whatever types of windows you install, be sure to insulate around the windows and rough framing openings. Although insulation is not intended to be compressed, you can cut heat and cooling loss by packing small strips of insulation into minute cracks. Use the blade of a screwdriver to force the insulation into the narrow cracks. Pack until no light penetrates the crack.

You also can buy spray insulation, which is forced into cracks where it expands to provide a perfect seal against weather. After the bead dries, cut off the part that extends past the wall line, and you have a neat appearance as well as good insulation.

Rowlock walls

Rowlock walls are a less watertight variety of cavity walls. Heat loss is also greater along header courses, although the face of the rowlock wall appears to be almost identical to a common bond wall with a header course every six or seven rows. The rowlock serves as a bond between wythes, partially replaces ties, and decreases the cavity depth. The cavity width for a single rowlock wall is about 2 inches, while that of a double rowlock wall (both wythes run with rowlock header courses) is about 4 inches (FIG. 6-3).

As with solid walls, brick is laid with corner leads, and follows the same procedures, including joint making, closures, and so on.

BRICKS WITH BEAMS

When beams for floors and ceilings must be set into brick walls, a few extra moves are needed. When an all-brick structure is going up, beams and joists must be set into the brick walls to provide platforms for floors and ceilings. In most cases, cavity walls are used for this type of construction to provide proper thermal and sound insulation. To keep mortar away from wood joists or beams, you may want to construct a beam box of pressure-treated lumber to hold the end of the joist or beam. Mortar, over time, may cause rot if it becomes, and remains, damp. You may also, of course, save the fabrication time and costs by using lightly pressure-treated lumber for joists and beams. I believe that homes constructed in termite-infested areas of the world should always use pressure-treated lumber for sills, floors joists, and low-level beams anyway. The few extra

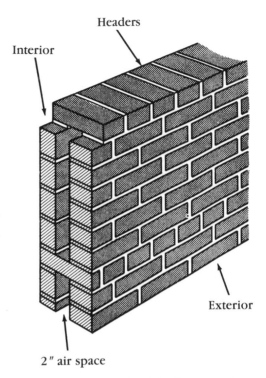

6-3 Rowlock walls use header courses to tie wythes together. The rowlock forms the bond between the two wythes and partially replaces brick ties.

dollars such treatment costs is almost always made up in the general savings gained by getting the better-quality lumber that most wood preserving companies use. Most treated lumber is Southern, or yellow pine, which is about the strongest softwood available. Its strength means you can usually use lighter timbers to span a gap or to otherwise support a load, but check local codes, the lumber, and Southern Forest Products Association load charts first.

Lightly treated lumber is classed as lumber having a 0.25 or 0.40 pounds per cubic foot retention rate. For ground contact and in-ground use, you want a minimum of 0.40. Even better is a retention rate of 0.60, and, in some areas, 1.00. Check brand ratings at various lumberyards to see what's readily available and what the manufacturer recommends.

Beams in solid brick home construction are cut at an angle, so that the joist or beam is narrower at the top than at the bottom. This oddity allows beams to drop free of the wall in a fire, limiting damage to the wall above and below the joist so that the house may be more easily rebuilt.

Joist anchors are placed at every fourth joist (no more than 8 feet on center, total), with 3/16-inch wall ties set into the first course below the joists. Joists above the metal anchors need solid *bridging* for stability.

For partition walls, indoors or out, a single wythe wall is adequate.

THIN BRICK WALLS

Exterior brick walls of a single wythe provide excellent divider and decorative walls, windbreaks, and area separators. Interior brick walls must be built only on well-supported floors: if you are planning a brick wall on the first floor of a house, you might need to install one or two extra support piers under floor beams. Check with a structural engineer before adding interior brick walls to existing structures.

Some single-wythe exterior walls work well when *piers* are placed at various points along the wall to provide a foundation. Using piers can save you a lot of digging for footings as well as the work—and expense—of providing full footings. If you live in an area where the frost depth exceeds 1 foot, consider such walls only if it is reinforced, and supported, on pier footings. All footing and foundation depths are determined by local frost depth levels, so you might need to provide a pier of only a foot in depth, or you might have to go down past 3 or even 4 feet in some locales. Make sure the local building inspector provides you with any frost depth information, plus local variations that might apply to your plans. After a structure is complete is not the time to discover that the foundation work is faulty!

Note, too, that footing width and length are determined by pier width and length. In most areas, a footing that is twice the width and twice the length is more than sufficient, but make sure you check. Some soils are better at supporting loads than others. Your locale might have the lesser supporting soils.

Start your brick fence by laying out the perimeter with stakes and string. Mark pier locations at the beginning and end of the fence, and at any corners. Stake those positions carefully. Next, mark and stake interior fence pier locations. Dig pier holes to the appropriate depth, width, and length, according to local codes and fence structure needs.

Place reinforcing rods in the correct numbers and sizes in each footing hole, making sure the rods are plumb. The rods should be driven into the ground for stability, but may be braced to save rod length (hardly worth the effort, as the cost of bracing is apt to be more than the cost of a foot or so of extra rod length).

Now fill the holes with concrete. Let it set, after making sure all vertical steel rods have stayed plumb (out of plumb reinforcing rods complicate laying brick in the piers).

The ground between the piers is scraped and tamped to as close to level as possible, and then a bed of mortar is laid there. Note the section drawing in FIG. 6-4. Make your own plan to indicate what brick goes where. It does simplify things (FIG. 6-5).

Lay piers as you lay the walls, and envelop the reinforcing rod in the piers with mortar as you go up. Make mortar a bit runnier than normal for those areas where reinforcing steel is laid. Steel bar or wire mesh is used on the first course of the brick, as well as in the piers, and is continued up the wall.

To lay a narrow brick wall without reinforcing steel or piers, you must have a poured footing. That footing will need to be 8 inches wide (for nominal 4-inch-wide brick) by 6 inches deep, but must be buried to frost depth or below, with any resulting foundation built up with concrete block. If a footing is used under block, the footing must be twice as

**Check local
building code
for allowable
height of screen**

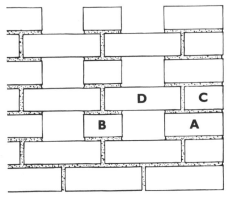

6-4 You can use poured footings or piers to support an outdoor brick screen, but be sure to check local codes and frost levels before you begin work. Brick Institute of America

**Construct
footing to suit
local building
code**

6-5 Planning your pattern of cut and full bricks makes the job much easier. Start by cutting a brick to 6 inches (A). Then cut a brick in half and center it on a lower joint (B). Start the next course with a half-brick (C) and continue with a full or stretcher brick (D). After the stretcher course is in place, repeat the pattern. Brick Institute of America

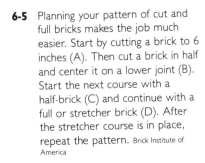

wide as the block used (you can buy and use 4-inch-wide concrete block, instead of using standard 8-inch block). With a straight wall with no reinforcing, use bond methods that provide a good physical bond. The running bond and variants of the common bond provide good strength when used with Type S mortar for extra wind resistance.

Chapter **7**

Patios
and walks

*P*aved patios and walks can be produced in a number of ways. Patios themselves are fine places to spend some outdoor time, though the idea of working with tons of masonry to produce a usable patio—or walk—makes the job seem far more difficult than it need be. Patios and walks can both be made with either soft-set or hard-set pavers.

The type of paver used doesn't provide much variance, but hard-set pavers must be set on a solid base, such as concrete. Hard-set pavers differ little from sand- or soft-set pavers. What is different is the installation method.

Hard-set pavers are installed over a poured concrete slab, set in mortar, so that they are held rigidly in place forever, or close to it. Soft-set pavers work differently, though the materials used as pavers are usually the same (few ceramic tiles are suitable for soft-set use, because they have little backing strength, but most other pavers work well: brick, slate, and bluestone, among others).

SOFT-SET PAVERS

The easiest method of producing new, flat surfaces of masonry is to use soft-set methods. Soft-set simply means the basic masonry units, whether brick or stone are not laid in mortar in a concrete pad base. They are laid in sand, on (if necessary) a gravel base.

Some essential rules govern this type of construction, and a few suggestions help produce a good-looking, durable job. The work is fairly simple and goes quickly and easily most of the time.

As with any job, a layout plan is a necessity, and I'll take that up in a second. First, though, examine the basic area to determine what sort of construction will work best. If heavy traffic is expected, one type will do. If moderate or light traffic is expected, another type is sufficient. Generally, for heavy traffic areas, you should go with full-thickness paving units, which means bricks about 2½ inches thick. A thicker sand pad is also needed, so you're working with at least 3 inches of sand, and gravel should be a layer of no less than 4 inches under the sand. A basic heavy-duty patio, drive, or walk, then, needs to be excavated to a depth of no less than 9½ inches.

For light-duty use, such as a basic sidewalk or patio that will not take vehicular traffic, you may use 1¼-inch paving brick, or even thinner stone, with only a 2-inch sand pad underneath, so enough give is provided to allow minute movements among the pavers when everything is finally locked in place (FIG. 7-1).

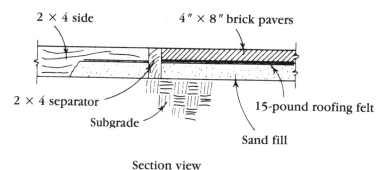

Section view

7-1   A brick sidewalk needs siding to contain the bricks and a layer of sand fill covered with roofing or patio felt underneath the bricks (or pavers). General Shale Products Corp.

Sand is an essential ingredient in all soft-set paving: sand under the pavers provides level support, and sand between the pavers locks the pavers in place between the borders.

At one time, bricklayers believed that soft-set brick pavers required a hard footing at the edges, using brick or other materials set into solid concrete. Today, any solidly set material, including landscaping timbers or railroad ties of redwood or other resistant woods, is considered capable of providing a practical boundary edge for soft-set pavers.

Within those borders, bricks or pavers can be laid out in a variety of patterns. Figure 7-2 shows possible 32-inch and 36-inch square patterns for bricks with a 4-×-8-inch face.

LAYING OUT PROJECTS

Find your starting point. All else works from here. Assemble *batter boards* for use in laying out larger areas. Batter boards consist of two pieces of 1 × 6 stock nailed solidly to three 2 × 4 spikes to create a square corner. Get a rough alignment from the starting point using a framing square and a tape measure, then move the batter boards at least 4 inches past the actual point and drive them into the ground. Repeat for all corners. Stretch lengths of mason's cord along the project's edges and tie to the 1 × 6s of the batter boards so that the cords cross at the actual corners

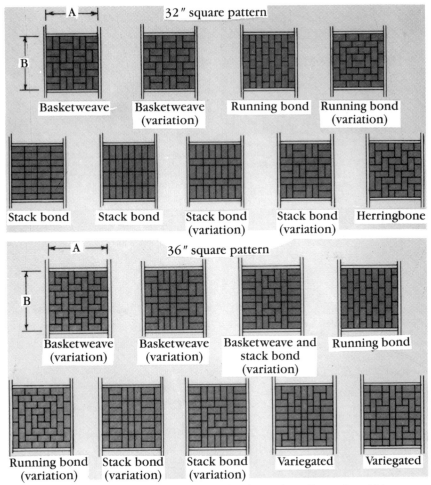

7-2 These patterns can be used in a variety of paving projects. Determine which pattern suits the exterior of your house and which dimensions best suit your needs before choosing one. General Shale Products Corp.

of the project. Check the inside corners for square with a framing square before solidly driving in the outside corner stakes. (Figures 7-12 through 7-16 illustrate the use of batter boards.) Square the entire unit using the diagonal measuring method. Measure one diagonal, then the other. If those measurements are equal, and accurate, the line is placed squarely. Otherwise, make adjustments on the batter boards until the diagonals match.

The mason's cord marks the actual backhoe digging point. A second line is added 4½ inches outside that after the backhoe has done its work. The second line is for the landscape timbers, where digging can be done by hand because the holes need to be only 3½ inches deep.

BUILDING PATIOS

Recently, my brother and I constructed a patio off my basement door (FIG. 7-3). We designed this patio to take light foot traffic, and the occasional

7-3 Before work began, the basement entrance area was poorly suited for heavy foot traffic and movement of appliances.

hand truck or similar item. (Sooner or later, washing machines, freezers, dryers, and other basement denizens of moderate size wear out and must be replaced, so we made allowances for that, even though we were working with appliances that were all under three years old.)

The area is badly drained, so instead of a simple 2-inch bed of sand, I felt a need to supply 10 inches of gravel underneath that. With a backhoe, we dug down $13^1/2$ inches over most of the area, up to 30 inches in one part and about 18 inches in another (FIG. 7-4). Then we dumped gravel and spread it out (FIG. 7-5).

Over the gravel, we placed patio cloth, overlapping each strip by 18 inches (FIG. 7-6). The day was windy, and we learned quickly that this lightweight cloth must be anchored with a shovelful or two of sand as soon as it's spread or it blows off.

You can substitute builder's felt, but the patio cloth is easier to use, and provides more effective drainage job since it is not impervious to water. Both materials keep weeds from growing up in the cracks between bricks.

With the patio cloth down, we dumped sand in nearly equal mounds around the patio, raked it as flat as we could, and then made screeds.

Screed boards are notched to fit at the ends of the patio. They are then drawn back and forth across the sand, leveling and packing the sand (FIG. 7-7). A screed is a 2 × 4 or 2 × 6 (depending on its length: for screeds over 12 feet, use a 2 × 6 and a helper) notched at both ends to fit down to the top of the sand layer. In this case, the notches had to be $1^1/4$ inches deep. We laid a trimmed 2 × 4 against the foundation wall, leveled in rela-

7-4 After we finished with the backhoe, the cleared area was level and ready for gravel.

7-5 After we dumped the gravel, we raked and smoothed the surface.

tion to the side landscape timbers, to give a surface to run the screed on at its back. We screeded in two steps, using a board notched on only one end first, then took out the center hump with a board notched on both ends.

7-6 Next we covered the gravel with patio cloth.

7-7 After we dumped sand on top of the patio cloth, we used a screed to smooth the sand.

Next you need to lay down sections of flat board, preferably plywood or waferboard, to work from without tearing up the packed sand surface too much. Stack bricks on the boards.

The pavers we used were General Shale's chestnut range paver brick with a standard face size of 4 × 8 inches. We made the edging with landscape timbers. This size brick works out to about five per square foot. Our final project size of 150 square feet needed a total of 750 bricks, about the contents of a single pallet of 1¹/₄-inch paver brick. We knew some brick would be wasted, so we bought a dozen or so extra.

We dug the excavation for the landscape timbers with a spade, after the major hole was cut out by a backhoe. The timbers were only 3 inches thick, so the digging was easy.

For the bricked area, 160 inches by 128 inches, inside the landscape timbers, we used a modified basketweave pattern with a 32-inch repeat. The landscape timbers added 9 inches in width and length. (An outline timber was used against the foundation wall; our timbers were 4¹/₂ inches wide.) An inch or two over on measurements is no problem, as that can be adjusted in the width and length of the pattern, changing gaps between bricks. Being significantly undersized is a problem. It is far easier to add ¹/₈ inch between bricks than it is to shave ¹/₈ inch off of bricks. We deliberately added 2 inches to the width and length to allow for variations in landscape timbers and brick. Final inside figures were 162 inches by 130 inches, with the overall dimensions 171 inches wide by 139 inches deep. Other patterns will give other dimensions, all of which may be adapted to suit any size patio, although 32-inch repeats require less brick trimming than do 36-inch repeats (partial repeat patterns need even more brick cutting). Try to arrange the patio size to suit, when possible.

Landscape timbers must not be cut too short. If you need a length like 171 inches, either timber of the two needed may be sliced off with a chainsaw or reciprocating saw, or half of the extra length may be taken off each. With a length like 139 inches, however, you must cut both pieces to provide the total length, rather than using one whole timber and one much shorter piece. The short timber will be too light, too easily moved by foot traffic. Both pieces should be reduced in length, with each piece at least 5 feet long, on the row next to the ground. Place the first rows of landscape timbers and repeat diagonal measurements to make sure nothing is out of adjustment.

Bore each timber to accept a 12-inch spike about 6 inches in from both ends. Use a ³/₈-×-12-inch drill bit in a ¹/₂-inch drill, or a heavy-duty ³/₈-inch drill (FIG. 7-8). Place the first timbers, then drive the spikes into the ground through the timbers, using a sledge hammer (FIG. 7-9). Check the level as you go and *shim* with cedar flat or shim stock if adjustments are necessary.

Next, start laying the pattern. We started at the left corner where the landscape timbers had been built up in several layers to hold a small bank.

7-8 To lay the landscape timbers, we drilled holes for spikes.

7-9 Next we used a maul to drive the spikes in place.

We used 18-inch rods to hold the stacked timbers securely in place, with reinforcing bars placed on 3-foot centers (or less), instead of just at timber ends, as with the spikes.

We used a modified basketweave pattern for a couple of reasons: it looks good, and a 32-inch repeat, with this pattern, means no brick cutting. We laid the bricks with a slight squirming motion to settle them into the sand (FIG. 7-10).

7-10 We laid the pavers in a basketweave pattern, standing on plywood to minimize disturbance to the sand.

Lay the pattern all along the wall of the house, and then on a perpendicular section along a landscape timber to make sure of fit. Neatness counts, but dead-on precision is unlikely. If layouts are precise with no odd angles at the other corners, everything will fit.

Lay all the brick. This is most easily done while kneeling on a 2-square-foot piece of 1/2-inch plywood. You might want to use knee pads, and gloves are handy.

Check all bricks for level. With a rubber mallet, tap down any that are not level.

Pour sand onto the patio, and use a broom to sweep it into the crevices (FIG. 7-11). Then hose down the patio in a sprinkle pattern and allow it to dry. It's ready for use. You may find, over time, that you need to come back with more sand and the mallet to make sure the bricks remain stable. Stability depends on how carefully the screeding and placing of brick was

7-11   Once the pavers were laid, we spread sand over the surface and swept it into the crevices between pavers.

done, and the patio will settle in a month or two in all but the worst cases.

With patios constructed in this manner, if for any reason a brick is broken, you can fix the problem in minutes by lifting out the broken brick and setting a new one down, after scraping away any sand built up under it. Then sweep sand down around it. If a brick is displaced, simply lift it out, clean out under it, and replace it, tapping with the rubber mallet.

These light patio bricks should not be driven on when used as soft-set pavers: if you're making a driveway you need full-depth pavers, or hard-set (set in masonry, on a masonry pad) pavers to take the pounding. For light use, such as one expects on a patio where lunch in the shade is to be the main event, soft-set pavers are cheaper and easier to install.

This project took two people four days, plus time to install a new rear entry door in the basement.

Now I'll show you a patio that's even easier to lay out than the first one. It is set out in the open, but also can be placed close to a house or other building. Start, as always, with the layout. This example took in 100 square feet, which required 475 bricks (4 × 8 inches, with a 5% waste allowance) and about 800 pounds of sand for a depth of at least 1 inch. A single roll of building felt will keep weeds from growing through, and you may select your own border materials. I suggest using pressure-treated wood (for ground contact, a minimum of 0.40 retention per cubic foot of wood, with 0.60 preferred) or heart redwood.

Outline your area with batter boards and mason's cord as shown in FIG. 7-12, and excavate to the depth of the brick you've selected, plus the

General Shale Products Corp.

7-12 Erect batter boards to help square the job, then excavate and level.

1-inch depth of the sand to be laid under the brick. Dig out about 3 inches past the expected finished boundary.

Place the borders and a temporary center form. To allow easy screeding, also keep one side and one end form temporary (FIG. 7-13). Fill the area with sand and screed using a board notched to the depth of the pavers. For best results, mist with a garden hose, tamp, and fill with more sand, screeding again until the surface is well compacted and very smooth (FIG. 7-14).

Now cover the sand with building felt, and lay the brick. (I prefer to use the sand on top of the felt for my work, though most directions say otherwise.) Lay a single run of brick along each of the permanent borders, as shown in FIG. 7-15, keeping the bricks snug against each other. Lay strings or chalk lines in 3-square-foot sections to allow you to keep brick aligned (FIG. 7-16). Fill in the remaining bricks.

Reposition the two temporary edge forms as permanent (this allows adjustment to fit bricks). Backfill.

Now stabilize the brick—bring in sand, sweep it into all the cracks, wet the area down, and sweep in more sand (FIG. 7-17). Repeat the sweeping and wetting process at least three times over the next week or 10 days to fully stabilize the brick.

Sweeping in a dry mortar mix instead of sand also works well for light-duty patios. Use a mortar mix such as that made by Quikrete. You can either hose it down or leave it until it rains. Make sure, before wetting, that all joints are well filled.

Finally, relax and enjoy, which is the whole point of patios (FIG. 7-18).

7-13 Put borders in place first, so that screeding will be easier.

7-14 After spreading and tamping the sand, screed it. Note that the notched ends of the timber allow the bottom of the screed to drop to the proper level.

7-15 Cover the sand with building felt. You can, if you prefer, use the felt under the sand. Then lay out two edges of the patio.

7-16 Use chalk lines to keep the first courses of bricks in alignment. Work your way across each chalked area and check alignment as you go.

General Shale Products Corp.

7-17 Spread sand on the surface and sweep it into the cracks. You might have to repeat this process several times.

General Shale Products Corp.

7-18 Your patio is ready for use.

OTHER SOFT-SET PAVER PROJECTS

Soft-set walks and drives work in pretty much the same manner as soft-set patios, with some minor differences. Walks are generally the easiest of the three to do, because the lightest materials are usually used, over a simple sand base. The basic difference is simply in the length of the project, as compared to the width. Once that's allowed for, the work goes much like setting a patio, though little excavation is necessary. If you use $1^1/4$-inch paving brick, and 2 inches of sand, with a patio cloth underlayer, then your total excavation needs to be only $3^1/4$ inches. (With landscape timbers as edging, measure timber thickness to check the depth needed at that point.) Make sure edging is firmly anchored, and go ahead and lay your chosen pattern.

Soft-set drives differ only slightly, too. Here, the difference is in the paver, which must be sturdy enough to support a large portion of a vehicle's weight without breaking. Full-thickness bricks are advisable, on at least a 3-inch sand base. Otherwise, techniques are the same, from layout to finish.

You need to remember, especially with drives where impact and pressure are both high, that exceptionally thin masonry materials do not take impact well; for all soft-set uses, avoid ceramic tiles. For soft-set driveways, avoid materials that are not a full thickness, preferably at least $1^1/2$ inches for stone and $2^1/2$ inches for brick.

Actual hard-set paver work is covered in chapter 8. Working with concrete slabs is an entirely different situation, sometimes requiring full-depth footings and many skills I've not covered yet. If hard-set units do not have footings, frost heave becomes a problem. In many areas, that's easily dealt with: pour a 12-inch-deep footing, and lay a 3-inch slab reinforced with bars or steel mesh. In other areas, you face major difficulty, because the footing may need to be 32, 36, or even 48 inches deep, which adds up to an impressive number of cubic yards of cement.

Such deep footings work theoretically, but in reality, I suggest going with 4-inch reinforced slabs, eliminating the need for footings if the slab is laid over crushed stone or gravel. This specialized type of concrete work is explained in chapter 8.

Once the slab is poured and cured, lay your pavers in a mortar bed, fill in between them with mortar.

STAIRS

Making stairs to lead from area to area in the yard, to connect patios, or be part of walkways is not difficult with soft-set paving methods.

Block the stairs in strongly, using landscape timbers or lengths of railroad tie spiked in place. Then fill leveled spots with gravel, patio cloth, and sand, before laying the first bricks. Outdoor staircases do not suffer as strongly from size limitations on tread width and riser height as indoor staircases do, but try to keep each step under $7^1/2$ inches in rise if possible. Keep the height of risers consistent throughout the staircase. Tread depth may vary from 11 inches to several feet, depending on your needs. Figure 7-19 illustrates more clearly how to construct your own brick-and-wood stairway outdoors. I'll discuss the construction of steps in more detail in chapter 9.

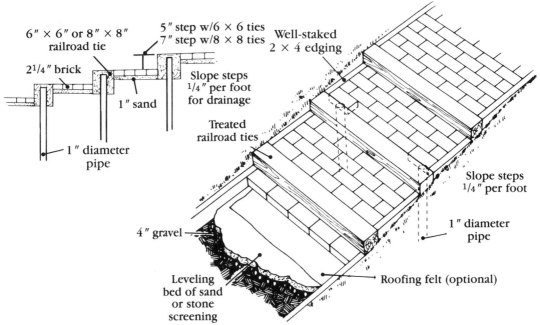

7-19 When constructing outdoor steps such as those illustrated, remember to slope the brick areas slightly to either side for drainage. The depth of the pipe depends on the condition of the soil.

Chapter **8**

Slabs
and pavers

*H*ard-set patios, walks, stairs, and driveways require more work to install than soft-set projects, but should reduce upkeep to a minimum for a good number of years. Although they reduce maintenance, hard-set patios require more initial work and expense than soft-set units. First, you must grade for a 4-inch slab with at least a 4-inch gravel bed to ensure good drainage and reduce the danger of frost heave. Then you must build the forms necessary for pouring that slab, lay in and wire together reinforcing steel, and provide the needed number of yards of concrete (FIG. 8-1 and FIG. 8-2).

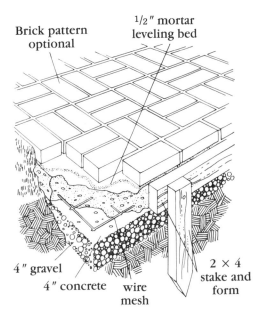

Brick pattern
optional

$1/2''$ mortar
leveling bed

8-1 Hard-set patios require a bed of gravel under a concrete slab reinforced with wire mesh and a $1/2$-inch bed of mortar. Brick Institute of America

$4''$ gravel

$4''$ concrete   wire
mesh

2×4
stake and
form

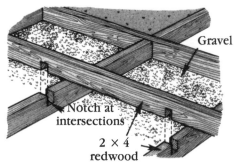

Gravel

Notch at intersections

2 × 4 redwood

8-2 A variation of a hard-set patio uses intersected redwood 2 × 4s as forms. Concrete is poured and brick is laid within each box.

From that point, you also use mortar to bed the pavers and bond them at their edges, but you get the advantage of being able to use any type of bond you desire. Hard-set paving is a lot of work, with a lot of initial cost, but the results may be worth it. Doing the job yourself, from layout through grouting the pavers, will save you about 50% of the overall cost of a similar job, which makes such work more affordable.

LAYOUT

Layout is done in the same manner as for any other flat job, working with stakes and a framing square to start, then going to batter boards, mason's cord, and diagonal measurements to get the final spotting.

You must first make absolutely sure you will have no access problems with such a patio. While it's relatively easy to lift sections of a soft-set patio, lifting sections of a mortared, or hard-set, patio, drive, or walk is difficult. You want to make sure that you aren't covering any water or dry well access spots, or any septic field or tank areas, and that run-off to the outside of the patio, walk, or drive is adequate. Simply leaving 1/8-inch slant per foot in any direction away from a house will not serve. The slant must be such that the water will not be channeled back to the house or another sensitive area.

Keep a close eye on deliveries, meter readers, and similar traffic, as well as on electrical, sewer, and water main entrances to the house in city and suburban areas. Avoiding septic lines, well lines, and telephone lines is also important in the country. You must not impede meter readers and others serving various utility outfits: if you want continued good cable TV service, for example, make sure you don't mortar over any of the connections.

Once all these factors have been taken into account, check the view, the shade or future shade, and similar requirements, in addition to locations near doors, requisite room access and so on. With a soft-set patio, you often might be able to shift the layout a few feet, or even yards, to meet such needs. Once a hard-set patio is planned and the slab poured, any shifting is exceptionally costly and a lot of hard work.

In other words, plan carefully. That's a good rule for any large job.

CEMENT MEASUREMENTS

Cubic yards can be easy figures to deal with, if you keep in mind that a 3-inch depth gives you a twelfth of a cubic yard per square yard of surface, while a 4-inch depth gives you a ninth of a cubic yard per square yard of surface. Such pours do not require a lot of material, and the 4-inch depth is preferable. For example, a patio about 12 × 18 feet, or 4 × 6 yards, has an area of 24 square yards. The total pour for a 3-inch depth would be 2 cubic yards, and a 4-inch pour would require 2²/³ cubic yards. While the difference is about 40%, the actual additional cost for the 4-inch pour would be minimal making a 3-inch pour, which has marginal strength, a poor bet.

As always, check local codes before starting such work. Where codes differ from my advice, follow the codes. With proper excavation and pour over about 4 inches of gravel (not a requirement in most areas, but it does help drainage and minimizes shifting), your concrete slab should be cured enough in 3 days to allow you to start bedding pavers in mortar.

When figuring the depth of excavation, you need to figure pour depth, gravel depth, paver thickness, and mortar bed thickness. The mortar bed can vary from ³/₈ to ⁵/₈ inch. A 4-inch gravel bed, with a 4-inch concrete slab, using a 2¹/₂-inch-thick brick on a ¹/₂-inch mortar bed, needs an excavation of 11 inches.

LAYING PAVERS IN MORTAR

The mortar bed goes on first, using mortar premix. Premix mortar comes in 40-, 60-, and 80-pound bags, saving a lot of measuring and extra lifting and lugging. You can make a mortar box of pressure-treated lumber or buy one. Commercial mortar boxes are good buys because they are durable, require little maintenance, and have curved bottom edges and corners so you can easily pull dry mortar out and get it mixed well with water.

While a garden hoe works adequately for mixing mortar, you'll find the job is easier with a mortar hoe: the holes in the blade allow material to pass through, and the blade is heavier and wider.

If you prefer to mix your own mortar, use type M, with 1 part Portland cement to ¹/₄ part lime and 3 parts clean sand. Whether you use a premix or prepare your own, start small, as the mortar sets up fairly quickly, and, as a beginning mason, you will not be setting a huge number of bricks at one time.

Allow yourself about half an hour from the time you finish mixing the mortar to mortar pavers. Begin with no more than two gallons of mortar, and increase the amount if that's not enough.

Lay edging pavers first. This technique simplifies some operations later, including alignment of rows in whatever bond pattern you choose. Use a string to indicate row alignment from the laid edging.

You'll need a level both to maintain level and to keep a check on the ¹/₈-inch-per-foot incline towards drain areas. Measure pitch with a 2-foot level that has a tapered shim along one edge. Make the tapered shim twice the height of your pitch. (The level is 2 feet long, twice the pitch length, so a 1/8-inch pitch will take a 1/4-inch shim, while 1/4-inch pitch will need a 1/2-inch shim. Use a 1/4-inch-per-foot pitch in areas subject to heavy rain.) Flip the level to check actual level.

After the slab has set up, make a dry run of your pattern, along at least two adjacent legs. If time and energy permit, make a dry run over the entire patio area.

If you have to cut pavers, make sure each paver used is fairly sizable. Tiny pieces are exceptionally hard to cut, mortar, and keep in place after the job is done.

If you're using brick pavers, hose down the brick. Brick is porous, and will draw too much water from the mortar if not wetted first. You want a damp, not dripping, surface, so hose the bricks down before mixing the mortar. They will air dry to about the right dampness within half an hour on most days. Do not wet down other pavers like slate or bluestone.

Mix the mortar and start laying the brick from a corner out, spreading a bed of mortar over an area you're sure you can cover in 30 minutes. For most of us, that's probably about 3 square feet at the outset, but personal techniques may make that area as small as 2 square feet, or as large as 6 square feet. You are better off laying down too small a mortar bed, and finishing up early, rather than too large a bed, with the mortar setting before the bricks can be laid.

If you did not lay the edging, you must mark the exact center of the patio and start laying bricks from there to the edges. With edging in place, start from one corner (after a careful dry run and thorough check for distance and size).

Butter the first few pavers where they butt against the edging. Once these bricks are in place, butter only adjacent edges. Bricks are shoved firmly in place against the one already in place. The trowel handle is used to tap bricks level in the mortar bed. If the brick is stubborn, use a rubber mallet to tap it into place. Cut off any excess mortar using the side of the trowel, just as if you were building a wall that lies flat.

Keep a running check on the level of the patio as you go along. You might want to keep a running check on mortar joint width, too, though minor variations shouldn't create too much of a problem. The pavers themselves are never really perfect. I like to keep a few spacers of 3/8-inch plywood on hand to help my eye (FIG. 8-3). Spreading half a dozen 3-×-6-×-3/8-inch pieces of plywood around the patio lets me grab one when I need it. I usually hold the plywood over the mortar joint to see if the joint is close to the correct width, rather than actually use it as a spacer.

When the mortar in the joints gets thumbprint-hard, it must be tooled (FIG. 8-4). You can use a storebought tool or make your own from a foot or so of copper tubing, kinked in a Z to fit your hand. Thumbprint-hard means what it says: the mortar is barely soft enough to take a thumbprint.

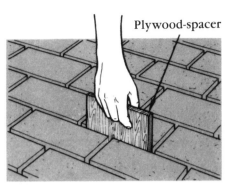

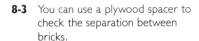

8-3 You can use a plywood spacer to check the separation between bricks.

8-4 Once the mortar has started to set, the final step is tooling.

At the end of each work session, clean up all the excess mortar you can. At the end of the job, you'll want to use either muriatic acid or UGL's Drylok Etch to clean up the worst mortar stains. Drylok Etch is safer to use and store than muriatic acid, but you still need to wear rubber gloves and eye protection and keep body parts well covered with old clothing. Take care in application so that you don't splash the liquid around (Drylok Etch comes dry and must be mixed). Some companies offer bricks with wax-coated faces that do not stain from mortar. You might want to check them out.

If you have trouble cutting brick in the traditional manner—with a mason's hammer and brick set—consider using a masonry cutting wheel. Do not use a wheel indoors if at all avoidable, and do use some type of dust protector. Don't expect such a wheel to continue cutting to the same depth as a circular saw. The blades, or wheels, fit in circular saws, but they are consumable, losing diameter as they cut away the material.

The abrasive wheels give a decent-looking finish cut with little effort, and require little skill for operation. You can also use them to cut ceramic tiles instead of buying or renting expensive ceramic-cutting machines.

Chapter 9

Projects

Now that I've described specific examples of patio installation, as well as general brick- and block-laying methods, I'll present a few reasonably simple projects that will let you practice what I've preached. You should try working with some of the smaller projects first, building to the larger, more complex ones. Once you've gained some experience, you might want to go on to larger projects of your own design.

BRICK STEPS

In addition to the projects in earlier chapters, you can overlay brick on concrete to relieve the appearance of plain concrete, both for walkways and for steps. Such a job requires the use of proper concrete step design and preparation, after which the bricks are laid on the cured concrete.

Making brick-over-concrete steps begins when you decide on riser-to-tread ratio and build the forms for the concrete. Review the various bond patterns and repeats in this book and decide how wide you want to make your steps. While outdoor concrete steps are often 48 inches wide, you can reduce that to fit a particular bond design or increase it to allow a full repeat of a particular design.

Once you decide on the width, you need to check about the need for landings (which must be at least 3 feet deep, and placed no more than every 5 feet in height, in a flight of outdoor steps). The top landing should be no more than 7 inches below the threshold of the door the landing serves. Pitch steps about $1/4$ inch per foot away from the building.

When figuring measurements for brick-covered steps, as in all brick-covered work, don't forget to allow for both the height of the bricks and the thickness of the mortar (FIG. 9-1). Bricks are usually $1^1/2$ to $2^1/2$ inches thick, while mortar beds vary from $1/4$ to $1/2$ inch, with $3/8$ inch considered a standard.

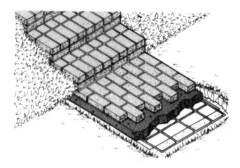

9-1 In excavating for brick-covered steps, consider the depth of the concrete slab, the bricks, and the mortar bed.

Risers must be in proportion to tread depth. If the riser is high, the tread is shorter. Thus, a 7- or 7½-inch riser should have a 10- or 11-inch tread depth, while a 4- to 4½-inch riser should have a tread depth of 18 to 19 inches (you virtually never find such low risers indoors, though they're not unusual outdoors: space considerations do not allow a staircase to spread out that far in most houses). Risers 5 to 5½ inches high will take treads 16 to 17 inches deep, while a riser of 6 to 6½ inches will need treads 14 to 15 inches deep.

Risers and treads must be uniform in any flight of stairs: the top, bottom, and all middle risers must be the same height, with the same tread depth. This uniformity helps prevent stumbling.

Level the base area for the flight of stairs, and clear all stones, loose dirt, grass, and other organic material. Use sand or gravel to get the site to a uniform grade, if needed, and then dampen and tamp the base.

Form building

Concrete form construction for stairs requires good bracing, and, at minimum, ½-inch CDX plywood. You can also use 2-inch lumber to construct the forms, but plywood braced with solid 2 × 4 or 2 × 6 lumber is both faster and cheaper.

Cut forms to fit, making sure they extend down far enough to allow for fill below ground level, and brace firmly in place with stakes made of 2 × 4s. Diagonal braces running across the tops of the forms are also needed and must be anchored securely to stakes set firmly in the ground (FIG. 9-2).

Use a level to make sure the forms are both plumb and level. For forms going up against a house or other structure, use a ½-inch bead of mastic to form a control or expansion joint. Coat the inside surfaces of the forms with used motor oil or a release agent to make removal easier.

When the forms are up, fill in any low areas with gravel, broken brick, or chunks of concrete block. Work the concrete mix in and around the rubble.

Mix all the concrete at the same time and pour. Use a shovel or the sharp end of a large pry bar to compact the mix and remove possible air pockets after slightly overfilling the forms.

Once the mix is compacted, screed immediately. Use a float or *darby* to level any ridges left after screeding and to fill any voids in the concrete.

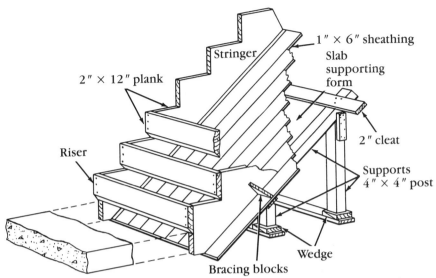

9-2 You'll need to build a stairway form, like this basic one, to pour the concrete for your steps.

Once the surface has lost its sheen, use an edging tool with a ¹/₂-inch radius to round the edges. Finally, give the concrete a final smoothing with a trowel, keeping the tool pressed flat against the concrete surface. Use a sweeping arc to trowel, with each swing overlapping half of the preceding one. For a textured, non-skid surface, use a wood float for the final troweling.

Concrete must cure and is best kept damp for three to four days during the curing process. Do not remove the side forms before it has cured for at least three days. If possible, let it cure longer. Once the cure is complete and the forms are off you can lay your brick.

Bricking up the steps

The actual bricklaying process begins with a dry run before you lay any brick permanently. Lay the brick dry to check fit and to see where, and how many, bricks need cutting or trimming. Do any cutting and trimming now, and make any other necessary adjustments.

Begin several hours before you want to lay the brick by hosing them down until water flows moderately off them. Such a soaking keeps the bricks from drawing water from the mortar too fast, a process that hurts the bond.

Mix your mortar, trying not to mix more than you'll use in an hour or an hour and a half. Lay down a mortar base about ¹/₂ inch thick and level it well with the trowel.

Pick up your dry-run bricks in an area no more than 12 square feet, and lay mortar on about half that.

Start with a brick in one corner and lay your pattern. Go on out to within 1 or 2 inches of the edge of the mortar before stopping. Lay another patch of mortar and repeat the process, picking up 8 to 12 square feet of brick from the dry pattern before laying down half that much mortar. As you progress, you'll get faster, and might want to pick up 16 or more square feet of dry pattern. Once you have a well-set pattern in front of you and are sure of your new speed and skill, go ahead.

Tap bricks into the mortar with either a wooden or rubber mallet or the handle of the trowel. Level about every third or fourth row of bricks: make sure you are keeping the brick graded at 1/4 inch per foot away from any structures. Use a shim on one end of the level (a 1/2-inch shim works well on a 2-foot level), and flip the level over to use the clear side for actually leveling across the walk, step, or other area.

Set a specific time goal for daily production and stop well short of that time. Then, using the trowel, pack freshly mixed mortar into the joints between the bricks. When the mortar sets to thumbprint-hard, come back with your concave jointing tool and pack the joints tightly.

After a few hours, vigorously scrub the surface of the bricks with a burlap rag to remove mortar stains. When finished, sweep well to remove dry mortar and other debris. If mortar stains are extensive, try DryLok Etch to remove them, making sure to follow all of the manufacturer's directions for both safety and effectiveness.

TREE WELLS

Trees may suffer two ways when building sites are graded or regraded. In some instances, roots become exposed as the ground is cut away. When dirt is added, anything more than 8 inches above the current height cuts off water, light, and air.

Tree wells provide solutions for both trees that are partially dug out and trees that are partially buried. A tree well is nothing more than a retaining wall, in one direction or another, so that cut-away ground doesn't remove dirt from too close to the tree, exposing the roots, or so that dirt being added to a site doesn't bury too much of the tree, weakening it through lack of nourishment (FIG. 9-3).

Start by using a rope or a garden hose to outline the needed size of the tree well. Use this line as the interior edge. Slip a piece of plywood under the hose or rope and mark the arc of the circle on the wood. Cut along that arc to form a template about 3 feet long.

Excavate a 16-inch-wide trench about 4 inches inside the arc formed by the hose or rope, making sure you get down several inches below frost line. Keep the bottom 6 inches of the trench smooth (curved footer forms are difficult to make).

Lay in a footer that is 6 inches deep and 16 inches wide. Screed it smooth and let it cure for at least a day.

Dry-lay two wythes of brick around the footer with 1/2-inch joints between bricks and wythes (use plywood spacers). Lay wythes in a horizontal running bond, so header courses do not extend through the wall.

Remove the bricks and mix your mortar, preparing only as much as you think you can use in about an hour. By now, you'll have timed your-

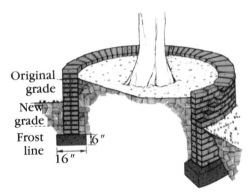

9-3 A raised tree well can protect a tree from exposure when the surrounding area has been regraded to a lower level.

Original grade
New grade
Frost line
16"
16"

self laying and picking up bricks and will have some idea of how fast you can go. Use that estimate as a starting point.

Spread a 1/2-inch mortar bed on the footer, and lay your first course in the mortar bed. Do not butter the head joints or the joints between the wythes. These joints are left open so moisture can escape, reducing wall cracking. Plumb and level each brick, and use the template to keep the well plumb from point to point.

Lay remaining rows using 1/2-inch bed joints, and a vertical running bond in each wythe. Plumb and level as you go up to ground level. Use metal brick ties to bond the wythes on every five or six courses. Use a convex jointing tool as the joints become thumbprint-hard.

Lay the top course with headers, buttering both sides of the bricks before laying them. Tool the joints flat to prevent moisture entry.

For sunken tree wells, prepare the site as for raised tree wells. The primary difference here is that all joints are mortared, and the exterior face of the well is *parged*, or back plastered, with cement up to the grade line. Either type, if needed, will protect a tree for many years and will also improve the looks of a yard.

ROUND BARBECUE

Barbecues are best located in the corner of a patio, when possible, but otherwise should be placed where access from kitchen and dining areas is simple and quick.

Mark a pit perimeter of 3 × 3 feet, and cut the walls of the hole cleanly enough to allow their use as form walls. Find a 22-inch-diameter form tube and set it centered in the hole. The form tube used must extend from the bottom of the hole to 26 1/2 inches above ground (FIG. 9-4).

Check plumb and level of the tube and then fill it with sand to about 2 inches below the final grade. Pour concrete around the outside of the base of the tube, filling the trench. Screed these footings and allow at least three days for curing.

When the footer has cured, start laying half bricks around the form with the cut ends facing out. Use 1/2-inch mortar joints. As you lay the half bricks, leave an opening for an ash door (the opening size will vary depending on the door you buy).

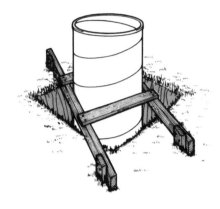

9-4   Use 2 × 4s to hold a round barbecue form in place. The form should extend 26½ inches above ground level.

After the third course is in, install a ³/₈-×-2-inch horizontal steel bar across the opening, as FIG. 9-5 shows. This bar provides support for the bricks above the opening. After the seventh course has been laid, drill three equally spaced ³/₈-inch-diameter holes in the form tube. Insert bent rods as shown and lay two more courses. Drill three more ³/₈-inch-diameter holes to act as grill supports; insert the supports and lay the final course of half bricks, completing the inside of the barbecue.

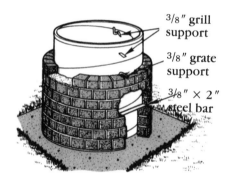

³/₈″ grill support

³/₈″ grate support

³/₈″ × 2″ steel bar

9-5   Use half bricks to create the inside wall of the barbecue. Leave space for an ash door as illustrated.

For the outside of the barbecue, lay the first wythe of a rectangular outside wall in a running bond. Go up four courses. Build the corners first (see chapter 10), and work toward the center of each side, keeping a check on level and plumb.

Make a set of 2 × 4 supports, as shown, and set them against the brick, tops flush with the tops of the fourth course. Lay a course of bull headers. Then build two wythes of stretchers in a running bond, two courses high (FIG. 9-6).

Lay a course of bull headers level with the height of the pit wall. As mortar joints become thumbprint-hard, finish them with a concave joint tool, and brush away any loose mortar bits. Strike top joints flat to reduce moisture entry.

After 24 hours, remove the wood supports. Peel the form tube down to the sand, and then smooth the sand. Lay in a 4-inch concrete bed, sloping it slightly towards the ash door for water drainage.

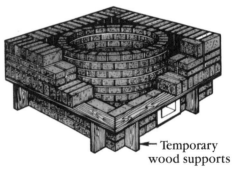

9-6 Install temporary wood supports to finish laying the exterior wall. You can remove the supports after 24 hours.

Temporary wood supports

Finally, fill the spaces between the interior and exterior walls with concrete, flush with the top courses (FIG. 9-7). Install the grate and grill.

Allow the concrete and mortar to cure for at least 10 days before using the barbecue.

9-7 As the final step, fill the space between the interior and exterior walls with concrete and allow to cure for 10 days.

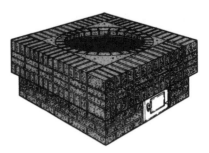

SANDBOX PLAY AREA

This easy-to-make project requires only a few bricks, some 1 × 4 pressure-treated and water-repellent boards, 5/8-inch exterior plywood, 1 × 3s and 2 × 2s, both pressure-treated, and sand.

Stake and dig an area 104³/4 inches square. Border that area with the 1 × 4 boards. You may wish to lay an inch or two of gravel; It's essential in wet areas (FIG. 9-8).

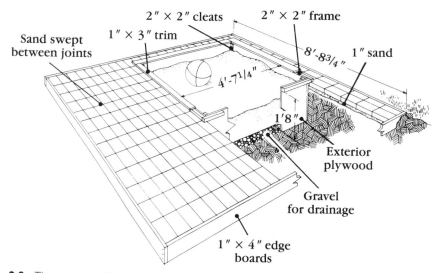

9-8   The area around this sandbox is constructed of soft-set pavers. Gravel under the sandbox allows for drainage.

Construct the sandbox of the exterior plywood (you can also buy pressure-treated plywood, which I recommend for this project) and 2 × 2 lumber. The inside dimensions of the square box made are 55¼ inches. Depth is 20 inches. The 2 × 2 is used as a top-mounted frame, along the outside top edge of the plywood, which is then capped with the 1 × 3 material.

Spread a layer of sand over the area not covered by the sandbox, tamp the surface smooth, and lay bricks in a stack pattern over the entire area not devoted to the sandbox. Tap the bricks into place with a rubber mallet.

Sweep sand into the cracks when you've completed laying the bricks, and the job is done (FIG. 9-9). You'll probably have to come back and fill with sand a few more times until the unit fully stabilizes.

STEPPING STONES

Brick stepping stones, in a frame of pressure-treated wood or heart redwood, can create an exceptionally attractive walk for a garden, and they are quick and easy to make.

Assemble a 2-foot level, a 4 × 4 or 4 × 6 that will serve as a tamper, a framing square, a spade, a claw hammer, a saw, a combination square, and a measuring tape. The materials you'll need to make 10 16-inch squares are 80 solid bricks, 3¾ × 2¼ × 8 inches; 10 6-foot lengths of 1 × 4 boards; a pound of 6d (6 penny) galvanized or aluminum nails; one bag of Portland cement; and about 260 pounds of sand.

Site your stepping stones, spacing them about 4 inches apart, and digging 4-inch-deep holes large enough to take a frame that will measure 17½ inches square on its outside. Cut four boards for each stone, each

9-9 The finished sandbox creates an attractive and useful play area.

board 16³/4 inches long. With two nails at each end, assemble and square the frames. Install the frames in the holes.

Mix the cement, 1 part cement to 3 parts sand, and spray the dry mixture 1¹/2 inches deep in each hole. Tap and add more to bring it near the frame level. Lay in the bricks so they are flush with the top of the frame (FIG. 9-10). The cement mix may be replaced by sand or readymix.

MORTARLESS BARBECUE

This unit goes up quickly and easily and may be taken down and moved almost as easily, yet it is sturdy, stable, and handy. Tools include a hand level, a length of 2 × 4, and gloves. Make sure the site is level. Buy the grill racks first, so the size can be adjusted to fit (FIG. 9-11). The unit pictured in FIG. 9-12 took 236 bricks, 3³/4 × 2¹/4 × 8 inches, and two grill racks.

Follow the pattern shown, carefully tapping in the grill-rack support bricks before moving on to adjacent work. Lay the 2 × 4 edgewise to the bricks being tapped and use a hammer.

MAILBOX SUPPORT

For this project, assemble a brick trowel, a 2-foot level, a jointing tool, a brick chisel, a mason's hammer, a pipe wrench, a measuring tape, and a spade. You'll need about 60 cored bricks, 3³/4 × 2¹/4 × 8 inches, and some ¹/4-inch steel pencil rod—two 4-inch, two 6-inch, and four 8-inch pieces. In addition, you'll need two pieces of ¹/2-inch reinforcing bar 53 inches long, approximately one bag of readymix mortar and enough readymix concrete to make 5.3 cubic feet for the footer.

9-10 Stepping stones are made easily from pavers and redwood timbers.

Make a 16-×-24-inch (16 inches back to front of the mailbox) footing hole. Check local codes for the frost depth so the box won't shift over time (FIG. 9-13).

The unit is built upside down, so you need to find a level workspace where it can stand for about a week. Use a plywood base if no driveway space is available. Make sure you work as close as possible to the final site—each post will weigh about 130 pounds.

Place and mortar the top course of bricks as shown in FIG. 9-13. Note that each post is built as a separate unit. Fill a core with mortar and insert one of the 4-inch bar lengths as shown. Cut a brick in half and lay and mortar with two full length bricks. Fill only those cores that receive 6-inch and 8-inch lengths of bar.

For the fourth course, cut a brick in half and lay a whole unit and half a unit. Fill the cores and insert the 1/2-inch bar. Now you must wait for at

Size of rack
determines size of
opening

32"   40"

9-11 This mortarless barbecue can be
built in a few hours. You can vary
the size of the work surface to
meet your needs. Brick Institute of
America

18"

Tap bricks in
slightly to support
grill racks

Size of work
surface
is optional

Brick Institute of America

9-12 The finished grill can be moved easily if the need arises.

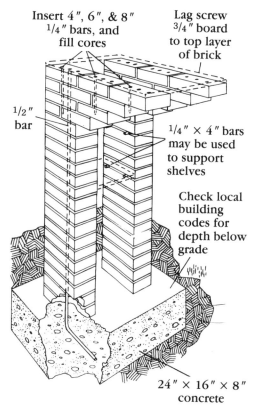

Insert 4″, 6″, & 8″ ¼″ bars, and fill cores

Lag screw ¾″ board to top layer of brick

½″ bar

¼″ × 4″ bars may be used to support shelves

Check local building codes for depth below grade

24″ × 16″ × 8″ concrete

9-13 This basic design for a mailbox post includes optional shelves. Check with local code officials for footing requirements before installing. Brick Institute of America

least four hours to let the mortar set around the ½-inch bar; if the bar is wiggled too much, the mortar won't bond to it.

Spread mortar and thread each brick over the ½-inch bar, filling in the core around the bar as each brick is laid. Support the posts and allow the mortar to set up for at least one week.

The next step is to set the posts in a concrete base. First, using the pipe wrench or a piece of pipe, bend the ends of each ½-inch bar to a 90° angle so the ends clear the bottom of the excavation. Set the posts in place, prop in all four directions, and plumb. Make sure the posts are set the desired width apart, check plumb one more time, and pour the concrete.

The concrete must set for at least two weeks. Keep the tops of the posts covered to protect the masonry from the weather.

Once the concrete has cured, drive wood plugs into the cores not filled with mortar and screw a pressure-treated wood board, sized to fit, to the wood plugs. Attach 1-×-2-inch wood furring strips to the board so that they will fit under the mailbox. Nail the mailbox flange, which extends down almost 1½ inches on most mailboxes, to these strips. Figure 9-14 shows the finished project.

9-14 Attach the mailbox to the post with a wood plank and furring strips.

Chapter **10**

Advanced bricklaying

*T*he cement sacks are in place, the sand is ready, and the wheelbarrow is standing by. Your garden hose, bucket, and hoe are all close at hand, and you've made a 3-foot-square mortar board and bought two trowels and a jointing tool. The yard seems overwhelmed by several thousand bricks and you're eager to get the projects rolling—learning, I hope, as you go.

Before you get started, check to see that you have the correct amounts of brick, sand, cement, and lime. In most cases, jobs aren't hard to figure. You will need to know how high and how long your wall or other structure will be. After that, decide what the thickness of your mortar joints will be and go to work to determine the amount of brick needed. If you underestimate on the mortar, sand, and lime by an appreciable amount, you easily can head for a building supply firm and pick up more. But brick may require a wait for delivery, sometimes as much as two weeks, a long delay for any job.

ESTIMATING MATERIALS

For purposes of example, I'll assume your wall is a single wythe one, using a brick height of 2¼ inches. The wall is to be 5 feet high and 20 feet long. You want to use a ³/₈-inch mortar joint. A simple calculation reveals that your wall needs to be 23 courses high, with an actual height of 5 feet, ³/₈ inch. That's about as close as you can get to 5 feet without adjusting a couple of mortar joints, which can be done, but isn't really necessary for a simple exterior wall. Divide the length (240 inches) by the nominal brick length (8 inches). Each course will be 30 bricks long. Multiply 30 bricks by 23 courses for a total of 690 bricks in the wall. With a waste allowance of 10%, you need about 760 bricks.

Mortar estimates are subject to more variation, since neat masons need less than sloppy masons and since so many different mortar mixes are possible. At a rough guess, the wall might take from two to three bags of Portland cement, with sand and lime in proportion to that. Extrapolate from this example to approximate amounts of materials for various wall sizes.

I'll assume all footings and foundation walls are in place for your brick wall and step right into the work of laying out a common bond brick wall. First, lay out the brick along the foundation without using mortar so you can make any necessary adjustments in head joint widths. In any masonry work using regular sized units, such as brick and concrete block, the corners should be laid first.

CORNERS

Laying corners is called laying leads. Lay the first courses of a wall dry. The leads then serve as guides for the construction of the remainder of the wall. Lay the mortar bed an inch deep with a slight furrow or groove down its center to receive the first course. The face tier is laid on the corners and each will be built up for six to eight courses, or to the next header course, whichever comes first. Normally, the next header course will fall within that range, but with common bond walls that are not heavily involved in structural support of anything beyond their own weight, the design of header courses is up to you.

Cut two three-quarter closures before laying the mortar bed. Place the first one, and butter the end of the other, butting it against the first (FIG. 10-1) to form your first head joint at the corner. This head joint should be 1/2 inch thick. Cut off excess mortar squeezed out of the joint and use either a plumb rule or level to check the level of these bricks. Make sure the face edges of the two bricks are flush with the foundation.

Butter the side of the next brick—brick *c* in FIG. 10-2—and lay it in place. Make its end flush with the foundation. Next, lay brick *d*. Check the levels of these four bricks. Check the level of most bricks laid in the corners as you go along, with emphasis on the lowest couple of courses. Such care is the basis for a good wall with straight mortar joints. Misjudging the level at this point can call for some truly drastic modifications of joints at a later point to return things to a level.

Once these four bricks are in place, cut the quarter closures—*e* and *f* in FIG. 10-2—and place them according to earlier directions for laying closure bricks (chapter 2). Check the level again after you cut off the excess mortar.

Now butter brick *g* along its face and lay it, cut off excess mortar, and repeat the process for the rest of the bricks along the first course of that corner. Run at least six bricks along both directions with a header course, four if you're laying a stretcher course.

With the header course laid, spread another 1-inch bed of mortar along the tops of the bricks after you check for level in both directions. Proceed to lay your stretcher course. To lay a stretcher course as the first course, in this type of double-wythe wall, lay both wythes before putting

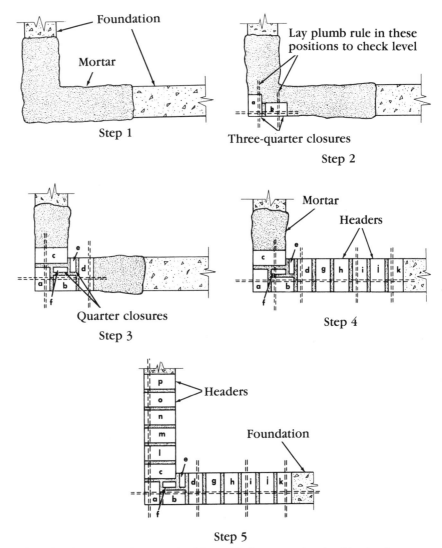

10-1   The first course of a corner lead for an 8-inch common bond wall is a header course. Start by laying out two three-quarter closures (bricks a and b).

in a header course above them. Lay the outside stretcher course first, carefully applying mortar to reduce spill onto parts of the course not yet covered (FIG. 10-2).

Use full brick on the stretcher course, and carry on the bricklaying procedure until the outside stretcher courses reach the height of the next header course. Then lay the inside stretcher course and the new header course just like the first. Continue the wall in the same manner, carefully checking that the corners are plumb (FIG. 10-3).

Tool the joints as soon as they get thumbprint hard. You can use a line, after the corners are in place, to help guide the wall level along its

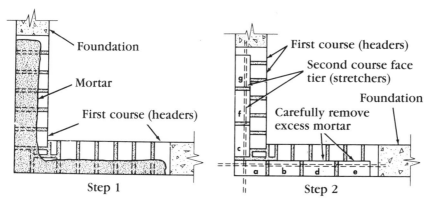

Step 1

Step 2

Three-quarter closures

Three-quarter closures

Step 3

10-2 The second course of an 8-inch common bond wall is a stretcher course. Mortar only the area to be covered by the stretcher bricks.

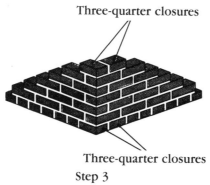

10-3 As the wall climbs in height, make regular checks for level and plumb accuracy. If a wall is off plumb by only a fraction of an inch near the bottom, the discrepancy can become serious at the top.

length (FIG. 10-4). The line saves checking every time you lay a couple of bricks. You can push a nail into a joint at each corner, wrap a mason's cord around two pieces of scrap brick, and hang it over the nails to serve as a line.

10-4   Use a line guide as you progress upward. Mason's cord is easy to use and can save corrections later in the project.

If you decide to make a 12-inch instead of an 8-inch common bond wall, things get somewhat more difficult. Lay both a header and stretcher course in the first course (FIG. 10-5). Once the first course is in, with three-quarter closures at the corners, lay a second course with the header course inside (FIG. 10-6). This procedure assumes the first course of headers was to the outside, which is not a requirement—your needs affect which course goes where. The third course may consist of three stretcher courses (FIG. 10-7), or the wall can now become a cavity wall.

The top of any brick wall will need protection at night. Use polyethylene sheeting to cover the wall with reasonable economy.

OPENINGS

If your brick wall will enclose a house or a portion of a building, you must leave openings for doors and windows. Normally, bricks are not cut to provide window openings. The top of one course becomes the base for the sill. The distance is easy to figure if you've already planned the height of window openings. Home construction usually keeps the tops of windows and doors at the same height to provide a clean line.

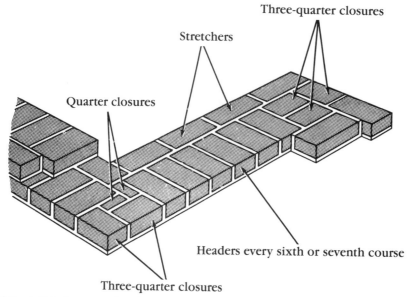

Three-quarter closures

Stretchers

Quarter closures

Headers every sixth or seventh course

Three-quarter closures

10-5 A 12-inch common bond wall starts with a two-tier course. The exterior tier is headers; the interior, stretchers.

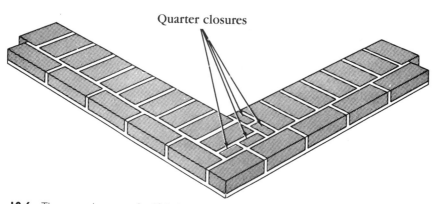

Quarter closures

10-6 The second course of a 12-inch common-bond wall uses stretchers on the outside.

The final sill course is a rowlock course, with bricks set on edge and angled downward (toward the outside of the wall) to provide drainage (FIG. 10-8). The rowlock course is normally set to take up, at the back edge, the same amount of space two regular courses take. Joints in window-sill rowlock courses must be carefully filled and tooled to ensure needed watertightness.

Once a rowlock course is in place, the window may be set in. Temporary bracing is needed for several days unless the courses are laid past a third of the window height. The bracing allows the mortar to set up properly. As you lay the courses around the window, take care with joints. The final window brick course must be no more than 1/4 inch above the top of

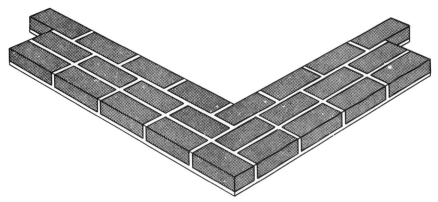

10-7 The third course of a 12-inch common bond wall consists of three stretcher tiers, with no closures.

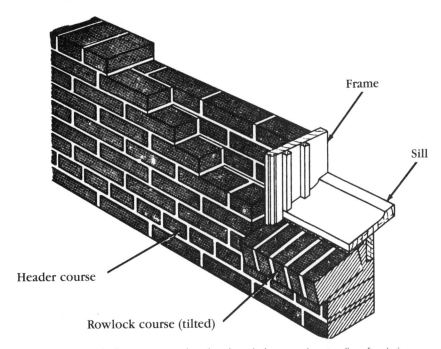

Frame

Sill

Header course

Rowlock course (tilted)

10-8 Tilted rowlock courses are placed under window openings to allow for drainage.

the frame. When you lay window openings in brick masonry, you must lay brick to the top of the windows before raising the corner leads, because you may need to make some adjustments to mortar joint thickness to get a correct top-of-window fit. Of course, you must also adjust the mortar joints down the courses to the corner lead, which means leaving the leads out until the windows are bricked to the top.

Lintels placed over the windows carry the load of the wall above them. You need only one try at opening a window with an improperly placed lintel, or no lintel, to realize what true futility is. The lintel ends rest on the final course of brick that is level with, or a quarter inch above, the top of the window frame. Lintel ends must be firmly embedded in mortar. Lintels, as FIGS. 10-9 and 10-10 show, are available in precast concrete and in steel. Use steel lintels where you don't want the appearance of concrete in a wall. Steel lintels can be hidden in a mortar joint. Sometimes you might find wood lintels. If perfectly made from pressure-treated wood, they are suitable. Imperfect wood lintels can be nearly as bad as no lintels.

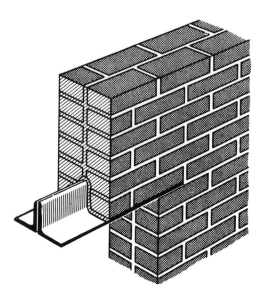

10-9 The legs of this two-angle steel lintel are each 1/4 inch thick so that the two legs projecting up fit exactly in the 1/2-inch joint between the two wythes of the wall.

Lintel size is determined by the span over the door or window frame and by the wall thickness. TABLE 10-1 shows some available sizes. Precast concrete lintels also come in proper sizes for the width and depth. Please remember that wood lintels are never used for doors or windows over 3 feet wide. The primary reason for the size limit is fire integrity. If a wood lintel more than 3 feet wide burns through, the wall above probably will collapse.

Table 10-1   Lintel Sizes

	Span						
Wall thickness	**3 feet**		**4 feet** *Steel angles*	**5 feet** *Steel angles*	**6 feet** *Steel angles*	**7 feet** *Steel angles*	**8 feet** *Steel angles*
	Steel angles	*Wood*					
8″	2-3×3×1/4	2×8 2-2×4	2-3×3×1/4	2-3×3×1/4	2-3^1/$_2$×3^1/$_2$×1/4	2-3^1/$_2$×3^1/$_2$×1/4	2-3^1/$_2$×3^1/$_2$×1/4
12″	2-3×3×1/4	2×12 2-2×6	2-3×3×1/4	2-3^1/$_2$×3^1/$_2$×1/4	2-3^1/$_2$×3^1/$_2$×1/4	2-4×-4×1/4	2-4×4×4^1/$_4$

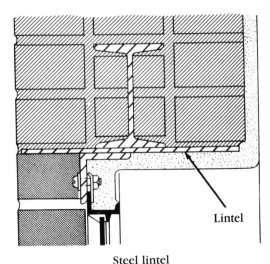

Steel lintel

10-10 Precast reinforced
concrete and steel lintels
are also available for
12-inch walls.

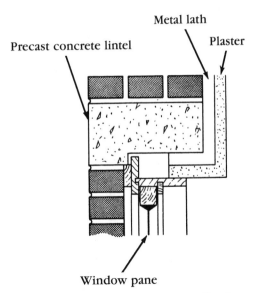

Precast reinforced concrete lintel

Door openings work in much the same way as window openings, but with much lower starting points for bricklaying. Generally, builders lay pieces of wood cut to the size of a half-closure brick in mortar to provide an anchor for the screws or nails used to hold the door frame in place. Wood used in such a way must be pressure-treated, though some building codes might not specify such a requirement. No less than five such blocks must be used on each side of a door frame to give strong anchorage and to allow for any needed leveling and plumbing (FIG. 10-11).

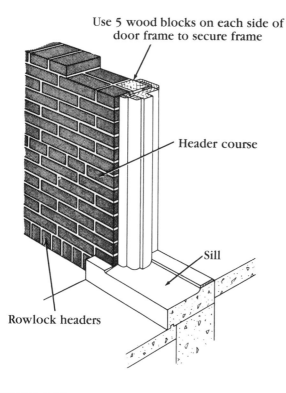

Use 5 wood blocks on each side of
door frame to secure frame

Header course

Sill

Rowlock headers

10-11 Note the use of rowlock headers at this door opening. Five wood blocks on each side of the door frame secure the frame.

CORBELING

Corbeling sounds fancy and looks fancy, but it's within the capabilities of most backyard bricklayers. Corbeling is simply setting courses of bricks out beyond the face of the courses, or course, below to form a self-supporting projection—a small-scale cantilever. Most often used in chimney construction, corbeling can provide extra weather resistance, decoration, and one or two other practical applications. A few simple rules must be followed.

Corbeling is best done with header courses so that greater bonding of the corbeled bricks is possible. The first corbeled course can be a stretcher course, if absolutely essential. The total distance a corbel projects must never be more than the total thickness of the original wall (FIG. 10-12).

Use care to tool and fill mortar joints properly when corbeling, so the wall retains as much strength as possible. If your wall must support heavy loads, and you strongly desire corbeling, consult an engineer to have the stresses figured correctly.

WATERTIGHT WALLS

Even with good bonding, masonry walls can be less water-resistant than you'd prefer. In most cases, lack of watertightness occurs in below-grade, or underground, masonry walls, not many of which will be made of

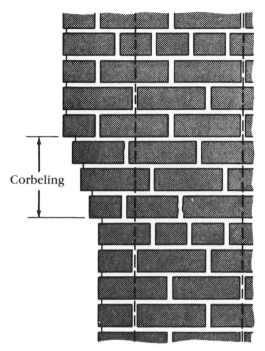

10-12 In corbeling, courses of bricks are set out beyond the face of the wall to form a self-supporting projection.

brick. In brick walls, water almost always moves through the mortar joints. With concrete block, the block itself might allow seepage. Head joints, rather than bed joints, are the likely source of seepage. The best solution is good bonding. Use bricks that are damp, but not dripping wet, with properly tooled joints. Above the grade, using sealing compounds might change the appearance of the brick.

With double-wythe walls where leakage might be a future problem, parging is a solution. The backs of the bricks in the face tier are parged, or coated, with a troweled-on, cement-rich mortar (FIG. 10-13). Parging, often called back plastering, lays on a coating at least $3/8$ inch thick. For parging to work, the mortar joints must be cut flush with the brick.

10-13 Parging, sometimes referred to as back plastering, is an effective way of leakproofing a wall. Before parging, you must cut mortar joints flush with the brick surface.

For a partially below-grade wall where water pressure may be severe, a combination of drainage tile, loose stone, and possibly, a membrane between the two wythes of the wall can prevent leakage. Drain tile, if used, must be at least 4 inches in diameter and well perforated (FIG. 10-14). Loose gravel may be used without the drain tile, though not as efficiently, so it is best used only where problems are, or are expected to be, minor.

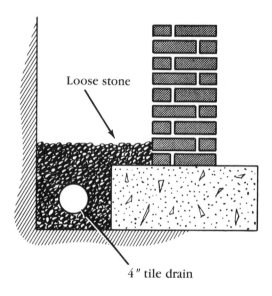

Loose stone

4" tile drain

10-14 A tile drain and loose stone help prevent leakage in walls below grade level.

Chapter **11**

Brick veneer

While brick cavity walls are among the sturdiest structures, brick veneer construction makes up by far the largest part of residential construction today. The reason is simple: cavity wall construction is more complex and more expensive than brick veneer construction. In many instances, it also takes longer. Veneering is simply the use of a single-wythe brick wall on the outside of a frame or block wall to provide a durable decorative surface that offers all the advantages of basic brick construction combined with the advantages of frame or block construction.

Brick veneer generally offers several advantages over conventional exterior sidings, solid brick walls, or cavity walls. Brick is durable and resists fire well. Sound transmission is reduced significantly because of the *discontinuous construction*. Brick veneer walls offer better thermal insulation than solid brick walls and slightly better thermal insulation than standard frame and wood-, vinyl-, or aluminum-sided walls. The extra 1-inch air space required in veneer construction adds a few points to the thermal resistance—and to resistance to sound transfer. Water penetration problems are low, if the wall is properly constructed; brick veneer walls are drainage-style walls unlikely to be afflicted with water penetration problems.

NEW CONSTRUCTION

Cost for brick veneer is a bit higher than for clapboard or other siding materials, but the use of only a single wythe of brick makes the walls less costly than cavity or solid brick construction. Brick veneer need not be restricted to new construction: old walls can be re-sided with brick with reasonable ease in many cases. Cost for such re-siding often may not be as much as the cost for re-siding with top-quality vinyl or aluminum.

For most veneers, the Brick Institute of America (BIA) recommends SW (severe weather) type of brick. The BIA also recommends type N mortar, which is highly resistant to weathering under adverse exposure conditions.

Foundation needs

Foundation construction for any brick veneer wall will depend largely on local codes and frost depths. In all cases, the foundation wall must be at least as wide as the thickness of the brick being used plus the thickness of the wall-stud framing or block. At one time, some locales did have codes that permitted an 8-inch foundation and footing wall (for single family dwellings) if the top of the wall was corbeled no more than 2 inches. In most cases, you'll find that the 8-inch foundation wall might stand but that the footing must be twice as wide as the foundation wall and poured to a depth of half its width. For a block foundation, you'll almost always need a footing 16 inches wide and 8 inches deep, set below the local frost depth. In most cases, the footing should be at least 12 inches deep; it's essential in sandy or loose soil.

Wider block walls are possible with standard 12-inch block. Such walls require 24-inch-wide, 12-inch-deep footings in most areas. These footings will also provide plenty of room for a standard framed wall ($3^1/2$-inch studs + $^7/16$- to $^3/4$-inch sheathing + $^1/2$-inch drywall), the 1-inch gap, and 4-inch brick.

Depending on codes, lumber types, and insulation needs of an area, you might wish to go out to a 2 × 6 (actual $1^1/2$ × $5^1/2$ inches) framed wall, allowing for 6 inches of insulation, with the studs placed on 24-inch centers instead of 16-inch centers. The cost is a little higher, but the added thermal insulation and quietness make it worthwhile if you can afford it. Using fewer studs also helps reduce heat loss—heat passes through the dead air in insulation much more slowly than through the solid wood of the studs.

Height limits

Even with proper foundations and footings, single-wythe brick-veneer walls are limited in height. For most residential work, you'll have no problem, since even 3-inch brick allows a wall height of two stories (20 feet). Using a full-width (4-inch) brick allows a wall height of 30 feet (TABLE 11-1).

Adding the veneer

Before the brick and mortar materials are delivered, you'll want to select a bond type for your veneer wall. Generally, any bond may be used, but try to stay away from stack bonds, which lack inherent structural integrity unless reinforcing steel is used. Stack bonds also tend to look boring.

As with cavity walls, ties used to connect the brick veneer to its backup wall are of great importance. They must be at least 22-gauge

Table 11-1 Height Limitations on Brick Veneer

Nominal thickness of brick veneer (inches)	*Stories*	*Height at plate (feet)*	*Height at gable (feet)*
3	2	20	28
4	3	30	38

Brick Institute of America

metal, galvanized, and no less than $7/8$ inch wide and 6 inches long. Use 8d (8 penny) galvanized nails to attach the ties to the backup wall. Your best bet is to nail the ties to studs or nailers. Deformed shank nails hold better (FIG. 11-1).

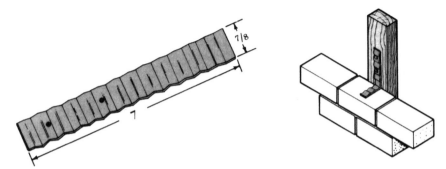

11-1 Wall ties nailed to studs provide reliable wall strength and support.

For block backup walls, nail the ties with hardened nails or with power-driven anchors. A number of power drivers are available, but the hardened nail is the quickest and most economical of all such block fasteners.

Space veneer ties at intervals of 16 inches horizontally and 24 inches vertically. At least 2 inches of the tie must be embedded in the mortar joint of the brick wall.

Use basic brick construction techniques to lay up brick-veneer walls, making sure that the gap between the framed wall and the brick wythe stays at 1 inch. The backup wall must be kept free of mortar and brick debris, though mortar joints must be full to produce a strong, good-looking veneer wall. Clean up back joints as you lay each row of brick to keep mortar from dropping and fouling the back wall.

Flashing

The veneer wall is a drain wall, so flashing and weep holes are installed to drain off any water that makes its way through the brick or mortar joints. Flashing is made of sheet metal, preferably aluminum—it is reasonable in cost and easy to use. Copper also works well but is quite expensive. Many codes also accept sheet plastics, but for a good wall, stick with corrosion-resistant metals. The money you save on cheaper flashing materials such as sheet plastic is not justifiable.

Secure the flashing to the backup wall and run it over the top of the first above-grade course of bricks. Any brickwork running below the flashing must be fully grouted to the height of the flashing. Position weepholes directly above the flashing, spaced on 24-inch centers. Weepholes may be formed in several ways. Simply leaving out the mortar in part of a head joint works. You might also use a forming material, such as an oiled rod, plastic tube, or rope wick. The plastic tubes and rope wicks are left in place after the mortar sets and are probably the two best bets, as they make certain the weepholes are open from the start (FIG. 11-2).

Windows and doors

The BIA recommends that you use steel lintels at least 1/4-inch thick for insertion of doors and windows in new brick veneer construction (FIGS. 11-3 through 11-5). Getting a good seal around doors and windows is imperative to cut out water and air leaks. Outside joints around window and door frames require accuracy. They must be at least 1/4-inch wide, but no more than 3/8-inch wide. Clean the joints to a depth of 3/4 inch and fill with a top-quality silicone-based caulk sealant. If possible, use a pressure gun to get the caulk down into the groove. If your joint is deeper than 3/4 inch, you'll have to use a compressible rope caulk before using the cartridge caulk. Use a V or concave mortar joint for brick veneer work.

ADDING VENEER ON EXISTING CONSTRUCTION

You also can gain brick veneer advantages for already standing buildings. The difficulty depends in part on the type of foundation and on the type of footing off that foundation. Deep foundations may require that you pour a new footing, while shallow foundations often allow brick to be laid on the front lip of the footing with no preparation beyond making sure an inch or so is available for dead space between the walls.

A single wythe of 3- or 4-inch-wide brick is not strong enough to hold up a collapsing house, so the stud wall behind the brick must be in good shape. The siding can be rough, as it means little to the finished job. Height limitations for brick veneer over existing walls are the same as for new brick veneer construction.

Usually, brick veneer is added to a home to cut down on exterior maintenance. Added benefits include the extra thermal insulation provided by the 1-inch air gap, and the added sound insulation. Generally, home value will also increase.

Foundation requirements

As I've already stated, the foundation needs for brick veneering on existing construction vary. If your present footing is reachable, in good condi-

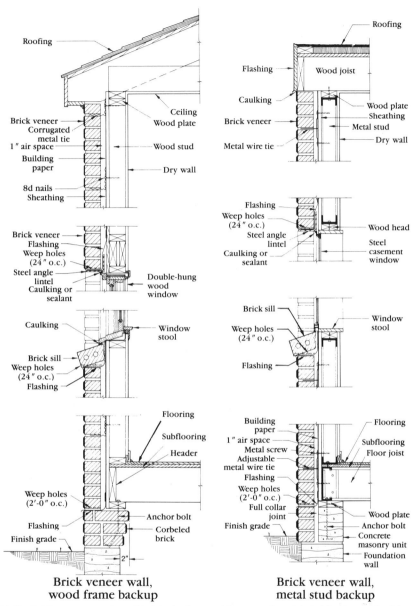

11-2 Brick veneer can be added to both wood-frame and metal-stud backup walls. Note the location and use of weep holes and flashing. Brick Institute of America

tion, and has enough front lip to allow you to add 3- or 4-inch brick with the requisite 1-inch air space, you might not need to make any foundation changes. Check local codes to be certain. If the footing isn't wide enough, you'll need to add some form of support. That support, in some locales, will be a new footing, bonded to the old footing, to support the wall's weight (FIG. 11-6).

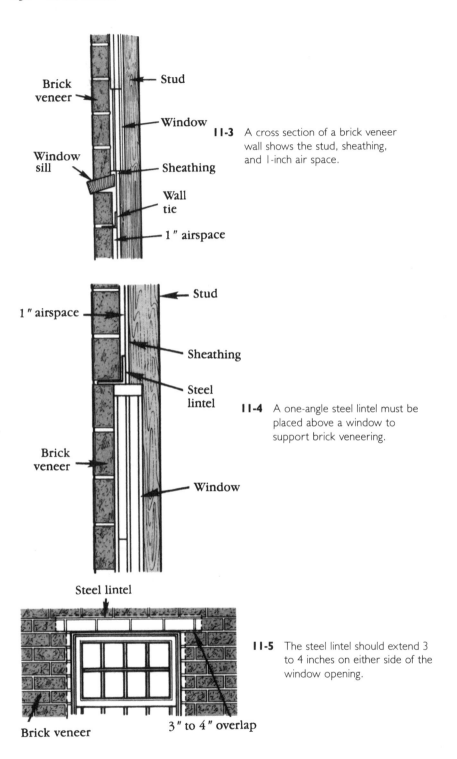

Brick
veneer

Stud

Window

Window
sill

Sheathing

Wall
tie

1″ airspace

11-3 A cross section of a brick veneer
wall shows the stud, sheathing,
and 1-inch air space.

1″ airspace

Stud

Sheathing

Steel
lintel

Brick
veneer

Window

11-4 A one-angle steel lintel must be
placed above a window to
support brick veneering.

Steel lintel

Brick veneer

3″ to 4″ overlap

11-5 The steel lintel should extend 3
to 4 inches on either side of the
window opening.

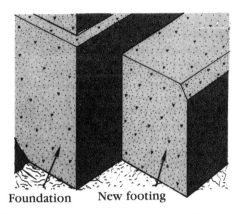

11-6 If the existing foundation is not wide enough to support brick veneer, you can widen it by adding a new footing.

Foundation   New footing

In other areas, you may be able to save excavation costs by bolting a steel plate onto the basement wall (FIG. 11-7). The plate must be wide enough to provide the appropriate support for 3- or 4-inch brick, plus the 1-inch air gap and must be mounted on the current basement wall with bolts that extend through the wall, backed by heavy steel plates. You'll probably need to hire a structural engineer to design the bolt pattern and layout for the project. The cost for the engineer should be a good deal less than the cost of excavating to full depth and coming back up with a wall of some kind, even half-width concrete block, after pouring a bonded footing on the old footing. Again, a check of local codes is always necessary.

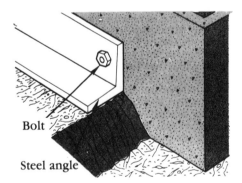

11-7 Instead of pouring a new footing, you might bolt a steel angle to the existing foundation to form an extension.

Bolt

Steel angle

For below-grade work, use type M mortar, 1 part Portland cement, 1/4 part hydrated lime, and 3 parts of sand. For above-grade work, use type N mortar, with 1 part Portland cement, 1 part hydrated lime, and 6 parts sand.

Laying the brick veneer

All trim that can come off around doors and windows should be removed, as should exterior light fixtures and electrical outlets. Porch railings and similar fittings will need to be resized, and new molding will be required around doors and windows. Place builder's paper over the clapboard or other siding to form a moisture barrier. Use at least 15-pound paper here (FIG. 11-8).

The 1-inch air gap isn't the only part of this type of veneering that is the same as other types. All flashing and weephole needs are the same as with new construction.

As the new brick veneer comes up under your eave overhang (cornice), the overhang will be reduced considerably in size. Before the new wall reaches 3 feet below the soffit and fascia, check and replace them as needed. If you come up too much farther, the job becomes difficult as you're forced to work in a cramped space. Use pressure-treated lumber here, because future rot would create major replacement problems with the brick veneer in place.

Caulk carefully. You now have a truly new appearance and feeling for your home.

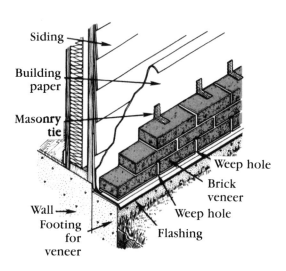

11-8 Building paper forms a moisture barrier between the existing wall and the brick veneer. Weep holes are also necessary to allow drainage.

Appendix **A**

Repairs to brick

*B*rick requires minimal repair over a period of two or three decades, short of actual physical damage from outside forces. Water might leak and create problems as well. Make sure all brick walls in a position to be susceptible to water penetration are properly constructed and you can avoid most problems. Where troubles do exist, installing open drains and new coatings of clear sealer can reduce problems.

After many years, brick can become discolored from airborne pollutants. Use sandblasting as a last resort after you've tried washing with extremely strong solvents. For exceptionally bad discoloration and stains of mortar or concrete on brick, use a substance such as DryLok Etch or muriatic acid, making sure to follow all of the manufacturer's directions for use and safety. Sandblasting reduces the water resistance of any brick, block, or other masonry wall, so you'll need to apply a clear or colored sealer immediately after the work is done.

Tuck pointing, or rejointing, may be needed on some walls. It requires some preparation. Clean out the old mortar as deeply as possible (at least 3/4 inch). Place new mortar, packing it very tightly, and tool when the mortar is thumbprint hard.

Damage is most likely to occur to individual bricks or to an array of bricks. If the damage occurs in a soft-set patio, you don't have much to do. Grab the required number of replacement bricks. (You did buy and store a few extras, didn't you?) Remove the damaged brick or bricks (FIG. A-1). Fill the depression with sand. Replace with an undamaged brick (or bricks), tapping into place with a rubber hammer. Check for level (FIG. A-2). Sweep sand into cracks to stabilize the repair (FIG. A-3).

When damage occurs to one or more bricks in a hard-set patio, break out the damaged area with a chisel and hammer (FIG. A-4). Clean up the area as well as possible. Remove mortar from undamaged bricks that were removed (FIG. A-5). Start laying new bricks in a mortar bed from an outside corner of the damaged area (FIG. A-6). Finally, strike the tops of the joints flat to reduce water penetration (FIG. A-7).

A-1 To repair loose, broken, or sunken pavers, first remove all defective pavers, including any that are not resting firmly on the base.

A-2 Check that the new level is even with the old level.

A-3   Spread sand over the area, sweep it into the cracks, moisten with a sprinkler or spray hose attachment, and repeat as necessary.

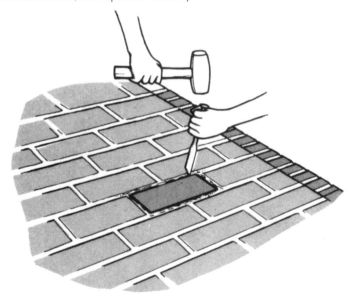

A-4   Use a hammer and chisel to remove hard-set pavers.

A-5 Clean old mortar from pavers with a hammer and chisel.

A-6 Butter the head joints of each paver before laying it.

A-7 Compress the mortar joints to prevent water seepage. When the joints are dry enough to be touched without damage, brush away any loose mortar particles.

Appendix **B**

Ladders and scaffolding

*B*asic scaffolding is simple and effective when working with masonry. In most cases, you'll require light scaffolding only a few feet high. If you're building projects for which you need taller, larger scaffold structures, be careful to follow all structural rigidity rules: bricks and mortar are very heavy.

LADDERS

Check your ladder to make sure it is in good condition. Wooden ladders should not be cracked or badly warped. Metal ladders with tears and twists need to be replaced. Fiberglass ladders are subject to both problems, but are so sturdy that only extreme abuse will do any harm (they cost proportionately more, naturally). Use only fiberglass ladders when working near powerlines.

Give thought to how your ladder is used. It must be set at an angle that is not too extreme in either direction, as FIG. B-1 shows. Extension ladders are more dangerous than stepladders, because you have farther to fall, and the extra length can get you in trouble with power lines. Keep all ladders well away from power lines.

Never use the top step on an extension ladder as a step. Go no higher than the next to the last step. And, of course, never use the tool platform as a step.

When standing on any ladder, always make sure your belt buckle does not move outside of the ladder side rails. In other words, don't lean.

SCAFFOLDING

The simplest site-made scaffolds are the best. I suggest you rent scaffolding for heights above those readily reached from simple foot scaffolds (FIG. B-2) or trestle scaffolds (FIG. B-3).

B-1 Take care to use the correct ladder angle when placing the ladder. A general rule of thumb is that the distance from the wall to the base of the ladder should be a quarter of the ladder length.

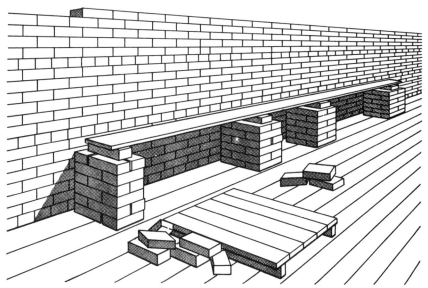

B-2 When you use a foot scaffold, create several piers of bricks or cement blocks and do not elevate the boards higher than 3 feet. Make sure your boards are strong enough to support the weight of masons and their equipment.

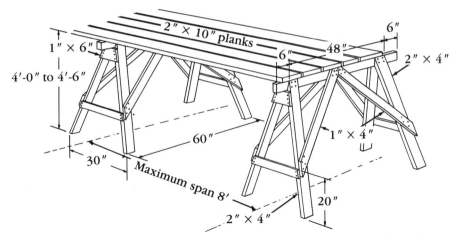

B-3 You can create a trestle scaffold with 2 × 10 planks and saw horses. Place the saw horses no more than 8 feet apart, and use sound, strong boards.

Appendix C

Brick Manufacturers

PRODUCT CODES

a. face brick
b. building (common) brick
c. glazed brick
d. pavers
e. flue liners
f. thin wall brick
g. floor tile
h. glazed structural tile
i. unglazed structural tile
j. chemical resistant
k. crushed brick

ACME BRICK CO.
Box 425
Fort Worth, TX 76101
(817) 332-4101
FAX (817) 390-2404
Products: a, b, d

AMERICAN EAGLE BRICK CO., INC.
Box 12786
El Paso, TX 79913
(505) 589-4474
FAX (505) 589-3071
Products: a, b, d, f

ASHE BRICK
Division of Boral Bricks, Inc.
Box 99
Van Wyck, SC 29744
(803) 286-5566
FAX (803) 286-9707
Products: a, b, d

ATHENS BRICK CO.
Box 70
Athens, TX 75751
(913) 675-2256
FAX (913) 675-7609
Products: a, b

ATKINSON BRICK CO.
13633 S. Central Ave.
Los Angeles, CA 90059
(213) 636-9846
FAX (213) 763-2434
Products: b, d, f

BALTIMORE BRICK
Division of Boral Bricks, Inc.
Box 72009
9009 Yellow Brick Rd.
Baltimore, MD 21237
(301) 682-6700
FAX (301) 687-7916
Products: a, b, d

BELDEN BRICK CO.
Box 20910
700 Tuscarawas St. W.
Canton, OH 44701
(216) 456-0031
FAX (216) 456-2694
Products: a, b, c, d, f, j

BICKERSTAFF CLAY PRODUCTS CO. INC.
Box 1178
Columbus, GA 31993
(205) 291-0930
FAX (205) 291-3237
Products: a, b, d

BORAL BRICKS, INC.
Box 1957 (13)
Arthern Rd.
Augusta, GA 30913
(404) 722-6831
FAX (404) 724-0302
Products: a, b, d, e

BOREN BRICK
Subsidiary of U.S. Brick, Inc.
Box 368
Pleasant Garden, NC 27313
(919) 674-2255
FAX (919) 674-5397
Products: a, d

BOWERSTON SHALE CO.
Box 199
515 Main St.
Bowerston, OH 44695
(614) 269-2921
FAX (614) 269-5456
Products: a, b, d, f, g, i, j

BRICK & TILE CORP. OF LAWRENCEVILLE
Box 45, Kalura St.
Lawrenceville, VA 23868
(804) 848-3151
FAX (804) 848-4000
Products: a, b, d, k

BURNS BRICK
Division of Boral Bricks, Inc.
Box 4787
711 10th St.
Macon, GA 31208
(912) 743-8621
FAX (912) 745-1289
Products: a, b, d

CAROLINA CERAMICS, INC.
9931 Two Notch Rd.
Columbia, SC 29223
(803) 788-1916
FAX (803) 736-5218
Products: a, d

CASTIC BRICK MANUFACTURING CO.
Box 8
32300 Old Ridge Route Rd.
Castaic, CA 91310
(805) 259-3066
FAX (805) 257-1253
Products: a, b, d, f, k

CHEROKEE BRICK & TILE CO.
Box 4567
3250 Waterville Rd.
Macon, GA 31213
(912) 781-6800
FAX (912) 781-6800
Products: a, b

CHEROKEE SANFORD GROUP, INC.
1600 Colon Rd.
Sanford, NC 27330
(919) 775-2121
FAX (919) 774-6634
or (919) 774-5300
Products: a, b, d, k

CHESTERTOWN BRICK CO.
Box 28
Chestertown, MD 21620
(301) 778-0878
FAX (301) 778-4392
Products: a, b, d, k

CLAYCRAFT CO.
Box 866
698 Morrison Rd.
Columbus, OH 43216
(614) 866-3300
FAX (614) 866-1210
Products: a, c, d

CLOUD CERAMICS
Box 369
Concordia, KS 66901
(913) 243-1284
FAX (913) 243-1287
Products: a, b

COLONIAL BRICK CORP.
Box 365
Cayuga, IN 47928
(317) 492-3355
Products: a, d

COLORADO BRICK CO.
Box 3513
6032 Valmont Rd.
Boulder, CO 80307
(303) 449-1227
FAX (303) 440-9228
Products: a, b, d, f, i

COLUMBIA BRICK WORKS, INC.
Box 1090
Gresham, OR 97030
(503) 665-9124
Products: a, b, d, f

COLUMBUS BRICK CO.
Box 9630
Columbus, MS 39705
(601) 328-4931
FAX (601) 328-4934
Products: a, b

COMMERCIAL BRICK CORP.
Box 1382
Wewoka, OK 74884
(405) 257-6613
FAX (405) 232-2726
Products: a, b

CONTINENTAL CLAY CO.
1441 Charles Town Rd.
Martinsburg, WV 25401
(304) 263-6974
FAX (304) 267-0793
Products: a, b

CONTINENTAL CLAY CO.
Box 1013
260 Oak Ave.
Kittanning, PA 16201
(412) 543-2611
FAX (412) 545-9659
Products: a, b, c, d, h, i

CORDELL BRICK CO., INC.
10538 Beaumont Hwy.
Houston, TX 77078
(713) 672-7531
Products: b

CRAYCROFT BRICK CO.
2301 W. Belmont Ave.
Fresno, CA 93728
(209) 268-5635
Products: a, b, d, g, i, k

CUNNINGHAM BRICK CO., INC.
RUR Route 2
Thomasville, NC 27360
(919) 472-6181
(800) 222-6476
FAX (919) 472-6181
Products: a, b, d, k

CUSHWA BRICK, INC.
Subsidiary of Steetley Brick, Inc.
Route 68 North
Box 160
Williamsport, MD 21795
(301) 223-7700
FAX (301) 223-6675
Products: a, b, d

DARLINGTON BRICK & CLAY PRODUCTS CO.
1910 Cochran Rd.
Manor Oak Building One
Pittsburgh, PA 15220
(412) 343-9993
FAX (412) 343-7270
Products: a, b, d

DELTA BRICK
Division of Boral Bricks, Inc.
Box 2
Route 4
Macon, MS 39341
(601) 726-4236
FAX (601) 726-2677
Products: a, b, d, e

DENVER BRICK CO.
Box 130
Castle Rock, CO 80104
(303) 688-6951
FAX (303) 688-5270
Products: a, d, f

D'HANIS BRICK & TILE CO.
Box 308
D'Hanis, TX 78850
(512) 363-7636
FAX (800) 299-9398
Products: a, b, d, g, i

ELGIN-BUTLER BRICK CO.
Box 1947
Austin, TX 78767
(512) 453-7366
FAX (512) 453-7473
Products: a, b, c, d, g, h, i, j

ENDICOTT CLAY PRODUCTS CO.
Box 17
Fairbury, NE 68352
(402) 729-3315
FAX (402) 729-5804
Products: a, b, d, f, g

EUREKA BRICK & TILE CO.
Box 379
Clarksville, AR 72830
(501) 754-3040
Products: a, b, d

FAIRHOPE CLAY PRODUCTS, INC.
12650 Clay City Rd.
Fairhope, AL 36532
(205) 928-8110
Products: a, d, g, i

FREEPORT BRICK CO.
Drawer F, Mill St.
Freeport, PA 16229
(412) 295-2111
FAX (412) 295-5210
Products: d, j

GALENA BRICK PRODUCTS, INC.
Box 368
Galena, OH 43021
(614) 965-1010
Products: a, b, d

GENERAL CLAY PRODUCTS CORP.
Box 16421
Columbus, OH 43216
(614) 486-0614
Products: a, d

GENERAL SHALE PRODUCTS CORP.
Box 3547, C.R.S.
3211 N. Roan St.
Johnson City, TN 37602
(615) 282-4661
FAX (615) 282-8767
Products: a, b, d

GEORGIA-CAROLINA BRICK
Division of Boral Bricks, Inc.
Box 1957(13)
New Savannah Rd.
Augusta, GA 30903
(404) 722-6831
FAX (404) 724-0302
Products: a, b, d

GLEASON BRICK
Division of Boral Bricks, Inc.
Box 72
Gleason, TN 38229
(901) 648-5527
FAX (901) 648-5912
Products: a, b, d

GLEN-GERY CORP.
Box 7001
1166 Spring St.
Wyomissing, PA 19610
(215) 374-4011
FAX (215) 374-1622
Products: a, b, c, d, f, g

GUIGNARD BRICK
Division of Boral Bricks, Inc.
Box 868
Hwy. 1 & Brick Yard Dr.
Lexington, SC 29072
(803) 356-1730
FAX (803) 356-2373
Products: a, b, d

HANFORD BRICK CO., INC.
Box 1215
Burlington, NC 27215
(919) 229-5811
Products: a, b

HARMAR BRICK, INC.
Subsidiary of Steetley Brick, Inc.
Rich Hill Rd.
Cheswick, PA 15024
(412) 828-6300
FAX (412) 828-6604
Products: a, b, d

HEBRON BRICK CO.
Box S
Hebron, ND 58638
(701) 878-4428
Products: a

HENDERSON BRICK
Division of Boral Bricks, Inc.
Box 2110
1309 Kilgore Dr.
Henderson, TX 75653
(903) 657-3505
FAX (903) 657-7139
Products: a, b, d

HENRY BRICK CO., INC.
Box 857
3409 Water Ave.
Selma, AL 36702
(205) 875-2600
FAX (205) 875-7842
Products: a, b, d

HIDDEN BRICK CO.
2610 Kauffman Ave.
Vancouver, WA 98660
(206) 696-4421
Products: a

HIGGINS BRICK CO.
Box 7000-167
Redondo Beach, CA 90277
(213) 772-2813
FAX (213) 540-0619
Products: a, b, d, f

HOPE BRICK WORKS, INC.
Box 663
Hope, AR 71801
(501) 777-2361
Products: a, b, d

INTERPACE INDUSTRIES, INC.
12502 132nd, NE
Kirkland, WA 98034
(206) 821-3773
FAX (206) 823-5555
Products: a, b, d

INTERSTATE BRICK CO.
9780 S. 5200 W.
West Jordan, UT 84088-5689
(801) 565-5200
FAX (801) 565-5220
Products: a, b, d, f

ISENHOUR BRICK & TILE CO.
Box 1249
Salisbury, NC 28145-1249
(704) 636-0131
or (800) 438-2002
FAX (800) 438-2002
Products: a, b, d

JENKINS BRICK CO., INC.
Box 91
Montgomery, AL 36101
(205) 834-2210
FAX (205) 265-0669
Products: a, b, d

K-F BRICK, INC.
Subsidiary of Steetley Brick, Inc.
Box 375
1440 John Fitch Blvd.
E. Windsor Hill, CT 06028
(203) 528-9421
FAX (203) 289-7485
Products: a, b, d

KANE-GONIC BRICK CORP.
Pickering Rd.
Gonic, NH 03839
(603) 332-2861
FAX (603) 742-8156
Products: a, b, d

KANSAS BRICK & TILE CO., INC.
Box 450
Hoisington, KS 67544
(316) 653-2157
FAX (316) 653-7609
Products: a, b, d

KASTEN CLAY PRODUCTS, INC.
Box 468
Jackson, MO 63755
(314) 243-3591
Products: a, b, d

KENTWOOD BRICK CO.
Drawer F, Hwy. 51 S.
Kentwood, LA 70444
(504) 229-7112
FAX (504) 229-3054
Products: a, b, d

KINGS MOUNTAIN BRICK
Division of KMG Minerals, Inc.
Box 729
Kings Mountain, NC 28086
(704) 739-3616
FAX (704) 739-7888
Products: a, d

LACHANCE BRICK CO.
Subsidiary of Morin Brick Co.
Gorham, ME 04038
(207) 839-3301
FAX (207) 784-2013
Products: a, d

LAKEWOOD BRICK & TILE CO.
1325 Jay St.
Lakewood, CO 80214
(303) 238-5313
FAX (303) 237-7737
Products: a, b, d, f

LAUREL BRICK
Division of Boral Bricks, Inc.
Box 583
No. 1 Brick Yard Dr.
Laurel, MS 39440
(601) 428-4364
FAX (404) 724-0302
Products: a, b, d

LEE BRICK & TILE CO., INC.
Box 1027
Sanford, NC 27331
(919) 774-4800
FAX (919) 774-7557
Products: a, b, d

KINNEY BRICK CO.
Box 1804
Albuquerque, NM 87103
(505) 877-4550
FAX (505) 877-4557
Products: a, b, d

KLAMATH FALLS BRICK & TILE CO.
Box 242
2420 Montelius St.
Klamath Falls, OR 97601
(503) 884-5419
FAX (503) 883-7105
Products: a, b, d, e, f

LEHIGH CLAY PRODUCTS, LTD.
608 S. 19th St.
W. Des Moines, IA 50265
(515) 225-7650
FAX (515) 225-1889
Products: a, b, d, e, j, k

LOUISVILLE BRICK CO.
Box 426
Hwy. 15 N
Louisville, MS 39339
(601) 773-5971
Products: a, b, d

MCAVOY VITRIFIED BRICK CO.
Box 468
Phoenixville, PA 19460
(215) 933-2932
FAX (215) 666-6277
Products: a, b, d

L. P. MCNEAR BRICK CO., INC.
Box 1380
San Rafael, CA 94915
(415) 454-6811
FAX (415) 459-1833
Products: b, c, d

MANGUM BRICK CO.
Box 296
2316 N. Louis Tittle
Mangum, OK 73554
(405) 782-2324
FAX (405) 782-5457
Products: a, b, d, k

MARION CERAMICS, INC.
Box 1134
Marion, SC 29571
(803) 423-1311
Products: d, f, g

MARSEILLES BRICK CO.
Box 306
Marseilles, IL 61341
(815) 795-6922
FAX (815) 795-6869
Products: a

MARYLAND CLAY PRODUCTS, INC.
Subsidiary of Cherokee Sanford Group, Inc.
7100 Muirkirk Rd.
Beltsville, MD 20705
(301) 953-2214
FAX (301) 498-3811
Products: a, b, d

MEDORA BRICK CO., INC.
1032 West Spring St.
Brownstown, IN 47220
(812) 358-4182
Products: a, b, d

MERRY BROTHERS BRICK
Division of Boral Bricks, Inc.
Box 1957 (13)
Arthern Rd.
Augusta, GA 30913
(404) 722-6831
FAX (404) 724-0302
Products: a, b, d

MINERAL WELLS CLAY PRODUCTS, INC.
Box 369
Mineral Wells, TX 76067
(817) 325-4808
Products: a

MORIN BRICK CO.
Danville, ME 04223
(207) 784-9375
FAX (207) 784-2013
Products: a, d

H. C. MUDDOX
4875 Bradshaw Rd.
Sacramento, CA 95827
(916) 364-5955
FAX (916) 362-9182
Products: a, b, d, e, f, g

MUTUAL MATERIALS CO.
Box 2009
605 119th Ave. NE
Bellevue, WA 98009
(206) 455-2869
FAX (206) 454-7732
Products: a, b, d, e, f, i

NASH BRICK CO.
Box 962
316 Earl St.
Rocky Mount, NC 27802
(919) 443-4965
(800) 662-6274
FAX (919) 443-4061
Products: a, b, d

NEW BRICK & TILE CO.
Box 1404
Dover Rd.
Easton, MD 21601
(301) 822-1420
FAX (301) 822-7271
Products: a, b, d

NEW DAVIDSON BRICK CO., INC.
24100 Orange Ave.
Perris, CA 92370
(714) 943-2911
FAX (714) 943-0588
Products: a, b, d, f

NEW LONDON BRICK WORKS
Box 257
Gold Hills, NC 28071
(704) 279-6901
Products: a, b, c, d, f

OCHS BRICK & TILE CO.
Box 106
Springfield, MN 56087
(507) 723-4221
FAX (507) 723-4223
Products: a

OKLAHOMA BRICK
Division of Boral Bricks, Inc.
Box 75368
4300 NW 10th St.
Oklahoma City, OK 73147
(405) 946-9711
FAX (405) 947-2660
Products: a, b, d

OLD CAROLINA BRICK CO.
Box 77, Route 9
Majolica Rd.
Salisbury, NC 28144
(704) 636-8850
FAX (704) 636-0000
Products: a, c, d, f, g

OLD VIRGINIA BRICK CO., INC.
Box 508
Salem, VA 24153
(703) 389-2357
FAX (703) 389-4716
Products: a, b, d

OMAHA BRICK WORKS, INC.
72nd & Main
Ralston, NE 68127
(402) 331-4477
Products: a, b, d, f, i, k

OWENSBORO BRICK & TILE CO., INC.
Box 907
Ewing Rd.
Owensboro, KY 42302
(502) 926-3330
Products: a, d, f, g

PACIFIC CLAY PRODUCTS, INC.
Box 549
Lake Elsinore, CA 92330
(714) 674-2131
FAX (714) 674-4909
Products: a, d, f

PALMETTO BRICK CO.
Box 430
Cheraw, SC 29520
(803) 537-7861
FAX (803) 537-4802
Products: a, b, d

PARAGON ARCHITECTURAL CERAMICS CORP.
2437 E. 53 St.
Los Angeles, CA 90058-3501
(213) 581-9888
FAX (213) 581-3840
Products: a, c, d, f, g

PHOENIX BRICK YARD
1814 S. 7th Ave.
Phoenix, AZ 85007
(602) 258-7158
Products: a, b, d, f, i

PINE HALL BRICK & PIPE CO.
Box 11044
2701 Shorefair Dr.
Winston-Salem, NC 27116
(919) 721-7500
FAX (919) 725-3940
Products: a, b, d, k

PORT COSTA MATERIALS, INC.
1800 Suiter St., Suite 570
Concord, CA 94520
(415) 602-1200
FAX (415) 687-1848
Products: b

POWELL & MINNOCK BRICK WORKS, INC.
Box 890
Coeymans, NY 12045
(518) 756-2164
FAX (518) 458-2881
Products: a, b, d

RAGLAND BRICK & TILE CO., INC.
Box 160
Ragland, AL 35131
(205) 472-2136
Products: a, b, d, g

REDFORD BRICK CO.
Division of Pine Hall Brick & Pipe Co.
Box 24096
12th & Maury Sts.
Richmond, VA 23224
(804) 232-6786
FAX (804) 231-3708
Products: a, b

RICHARDS BRICK CO.
Box 407
234 Springer Ave.
Edwardsville, IL 62025
(618) 656-0230
Products: a, b

RICHLAND MOULDED BRICK CO.
Box 1711
Mansfield, OH 44901
(419) 524-0000
FAX (419) 524-6611
Products: a,b, c, d, f, j

RICHTEX CORP.
Subsidiary of U.S. Brick, Inc.
Box 3307
Columbia, SC 29230
(803) 786-1260
FAX (803) 786-9703
Products: a, b, d

ROBINSON BRICK CO.
1845 W. Dartmouth Ave.
Box 5243
Denver, CO 80217
(303) 781-9002
FAX (303) 781-1818
Products: a

SALISBURY BRICK CORP.
Box 769
Hwy. 78
Summerville, SC 29484
(803) 821-1576
(800) 544-7933
FAX (803) 871-4480
Products: a, b

SANDKUL TILE CO.
5536 Kossuth-Amanda Rd.
Spencerville, OH 45887
(419) 647-4131
FAX (419) 647-6590
Products: e, k

SIOUX CITY BRICK & TILE
Box 807
Sioux City, IA 51102
(712) 258-6571
FAX (712) 252-3215
Products: a, d, g, h, k

SOUTHERN BRICK CO., INC.
Box 208
Newberry Hwy.
Ninety Six, SC 29666
(803) 543-3211
FAX (803) 543-3575
Products; a, b, d

SOUTHERN BRICK & TILE CO., INC.
Box 328
Byhalia, MS 38611
(601) 838-2141
Products: a, b, d

ST. JOE BRICK WORKS, INC.
Box 400
Hwy. 11 at St. Joe Rd.
Slidell, LA 70459
(504) 863-6161
Products: a, d

STARK CERAMICS, INC.
Box 8880
Canton, OH 44711
(216) 488-1211
FAX (216) 488-0333
Products: a, c, h, i

STATESVILLE BRICK CO.
Box 471
Statesville, NC 28677
(704) 872-4123
FAX (704) 872-4125
Products: a

STEETLEY BRICK, INC.
Rich Hill Rd.
Cheswick, PA 15024
(412) 828-6300
FAX (412) 828-6604
Products: a, b, d

STILES & HART BRICK CO.
Box 367
Cook St.
Bridgewater, MA 02324
(508) 697-6928
Products: a, b, d, g

STONE CREEK BRICK CO.
Box 116
Stone Creek, OH 43840
(216) 339-5511
FAX (216) 339-1736
Products: a, b, d

STREATOR BRICK SYSTEMS, INC.
Box E
West End of 9th St.
Streator, IL 61364
(815) 672-2106
FAX (815) 673-1749
Products: a, b, d

SUMMIT BRICK & TILE CO.
Box 533
13th & Erie Sts.
Pueblo, CO 81002
(719) 542-8278
FAX (719) 542-5243
Products: a, b, d, f, g, i

TAYLOR CLAY PRODUCTS CO.
Box 2128
Salisbury, NC 28144
(704) 636-2411
FAX (704) 636-2413
Products: a, b, d, g, f

TEXAS CLAY INDUSTRIES
Box 469
Malakoff, TX 75148
(214) 489-1331
FAX (214) 489-2480
Products: a

TRIANGLE BRICK CO.
6523 Apex Rd.
Durham, NC 27713
(919) 544-1796
FAX (919) 544-3904
Products: a, b, d

TRI-STATE BRICK & TILE CO., INC.
Box 31768
2050 Forest Ave.
Jackson, MS 39286
(601) 981-1410
FAX (601) 366-2205
Products: a, b, d, e, g

U.S. BRICK, INC.
Box 668
2121 Britannia Rd.
Streetsville, Ontario
L5M 2C3 Canada
(416) 821-4521
FAX (416) 821-7959
Products: a, b, d, e, f

WACCAMAW CLAY PRODUCTS CO., INC.
3300 Waccamaw Blvd.
Myrtle Beach, SC 29577
(803) 236-2121
Products: a, b, c, d, e, g, h, i

WATKINS BRICK & TILE CORP.
Ensley Station, Drawer B
Birmingham, AL 35218
(205) 786-4317
FAX (205) 786-7009
Products: a, b, d, f, g, j

WATSONTOWN BRICK CO.
Box 68
R.D. 2, Route 405
Watsontown, PA 17777
(717) 538-2555
FAX (717) 538-5903
Products: a, b, d, j, k

WHEELER BRICK CO., INC.
Hwy. 63B West
Box 250
Jonesboro, AR 72403
(501) 935-5182
Products: a, d

YADKIN BRICK CO.
Box 50
Route #2
New London, NC 28127
(704) 463-7353
Products: a, b, k

YANKEE HILL BRICK MANUFACTURING CO.
3705 S. Coddington Ave.
Lincoln, NE 68522
(402) 477-6663
FAX (402) 477-2832
Products: a, d

Glossary

adobe Brick made of sun-dried earth and straw.

American bond A masonry bond with a course of headers after every five or six courses of stretchers. Also called common bond.

base joint Mortar spread over a foundation or footing surface in which the first course of bricks or blocks is laid.

bat Half of a brick.

batter boards Boards positioned outside the corner of an excavation to outline and square a large area before masonry work begins.

bed joint See base joint.

blind header A bat used as a header, primarily for decorative purposes.

bolster A chisel used to shape or cut bricks.

bond The systematic lapping of masonry units to enhance strength and appearance.

brick Building or paving material made by baking or burning molded clay into blocks.

brick veneer Brick facing bonded to a wall built with another material.

bridging Metal or wood partitions placed between joists for stability.

building brick Common brick made of standard clay or shale with no special markings, color, or surface texture.

bull header A rowlock brick laid with its longest side perpendicular to the face of the wall.

bull stretcher A rowlock brick laid with its longest side parallel to the face of the wall.

burning One of six stages in brickmaking, in which brick is processed in a kiln at temperatures from 100 to 140°F.

buttering Spreading a layer of mortar on the end of a brick before laying.

cavity wall A masonry wall built in two thicknesses separated by an air space designed to provide thermal insulation.

clinker brick Brick that has been overburned in the kiln.

closure The last masonry unit in a course.

common bond See American bond.

control joint A continuous vertical joint that permits limited movement within the wall.

corbeling Setting courses of brick out beyond the face of the wall to form a self-supporting projection.

cored brick Brick with holes cut out of the center to reduce weight.

course A continuous row of bricks.

cross joint The joint between two bricks in a header course tying two wythes together.

darby A float used to level ridges or fill voids in poured concrete.

discontinuous construction The use of different kinds of materials in wall construction to break up the flow of heat or sound through one material. Brick veneer on a wood frame is an example of discontinuous construction.

drawing   The process of removing bricks from the kiln.

dry-press   The process of making bricks used when the clay has low plasticity. The dry-press process uses a minimum amount of water.

Dutch bond   See English cross bond.

efflorescence   The formation of a powder or incrustation on a masonry surface due to the capillary action of soluble ground salts.

English bond   A masonry bond in which header courses alternate with stretcher courses.

English brick   Brick larger than the U.S. standard, measuring 3 × 4^1/$_2$ × 9 inches.

English cross bond   A variation on the English bond, in which vertical joints are centered over the stretchers in the course below.

European brick   Imported brick with comparable strength and durability to American clay brick.

face brick   High-quality brick used on exposed surfaces. Available in a variety of colors.

fire brick   Specially treated, heat-resistant brick used to line fireplaces, barbecues, and other areas exposed to open flame.

fire clay   Deep-mined clay with refractory properties.

flashing   Material, usually noncorrosive metal, used to move moisture away from masonry vulnerable to water penetration.

Flemish bond   A masonry bond that alternates headers and stretchers on each course so that each header is centered above and below a stretcher.

flue   Air channel in a chimney to convey flame and smoke to the outside.

glazed brick   Brick with a ceramic coating applied to one surface, available in a variety of colors.

hard-set pavers   Basic masonry units laid in mortar over a concrete base.

head joint   Vertical mortar between the ends of two bricks in a course.

header   A brick laid sideways so that only the end shows in the course.

kiln   The oven in which brick is baked or burned.

king closure   A brick cut at an angle across one corner.

lime   An ingredient in mortar and cement that, combined with water, forms calcium carbonate.

masonry   Construction of almost any structure using bricks or cement blocks of uniform size laid in courses with mortar joints.

mortar bond   Adhesion of mortar to bricks, tiles, cement blocks, or reinforcements.

Norman brick   Brick larger than U.S. standard, measuring 2^3/$_4$ × 4 × 12 inches.

parging   Spreading a thin layer of mortar over a masonry wall. Also called back plastering.

pattern bond   The formation of bricks and mortar joints in the face of a wall.

paver brick   Brick that is half the thickness of regular brick, used for patios and walks.

pier A vertical structural support or an auxiliary mass of masonry used to stiffen a wall.

pilaster A rectangular column connected to a wall for reinforcement.

pointing A method of drawing a jointing tool along a mortar joint to compact the mortar.

pressed brick Brick made by dry-press process, having smooth faces, sharp edges, and square corners.

quarter closure One-fourth of a brick.

queen closure A brick cut in half lengthwise.

retempering The process of remixing and refreshing mortar.

Roman brick A brick measuring $1^{1}/_{2} \times 4 \times 12$ inches.

rowlock A brick laid on its edge as a header.

running bond A masonry bond in which stretcher bricks are laid halfway across the stretcher bricks in the course below.

sand-lime brick Bricks used extensively in Germany, made from a thin mixture of slaked lime and fine siliceous sand molded under pressure and hardened by steam.

screed A straight-edged board used to smooth concrete or sand.

shim A thin, often tapered, piece of wood or metal used to level an uneven surface or produce a drainage slope underneath masonry units.

slump cone A metal form used to measure the amount of slump, or collapse, in concrete mixtures.

slump test A method of determining the amount of slump, or collapse, in a concrete mixture.

soft-mud process A method of brickmaking used when the clay contains a high percentage of natural water.

soft-set pavers Basic masonry units laid in sand.

soldier A brick laid vertically so that its narrow face is exposed.

spalling Chipping and flaking of concrete surfaces.

split A brick cut in half along its depth.

stack bond Masonry units positioned directly on top of each other so that horizontal and vertical joints are continuous. A stack bond is the weakest structural bond.

standard brick A U.S. brick that is $2^{1}/_{2} \times 3^{3}/_{4} \times 8$ inches in size.

starter brick The first brick laid in each course.

stiff-mud process A method of brickmaking used when the clay can be mixed with enough water to produce plasticity.

story pole A rod equal in height to one story of a building and marked to indicate specific heights.

stretcher brick A masonry unit laid with its length parallel to the face of the wall.

structural bond The method by which individual masonry units are interlocked to become a single structure.

tensile strength The resistance of a material to twisting stress.

three-quarter closure Three-fourths of a brick.

wale A horizontal timber used to brace vertical members of a form.

winning A mining procedure in which several days of production material is held in storage.

wythe A continuous vertical tier of masonry.

Index